The Overload Solution

The Overload Solution

Jane Alexander

PIATKUS

✿ *Visit the Piatkus website!*

Piatkus publishes a wide range of best-selling fiction and non-fiction, including books on health, mind, body & spirit, sex, self-help, cookery, biography and the paranormal.

If you want to:
- read descriptions of our popular titles
- buy our books over the internet
- take advantage of our special offers
- enter our monthly competition
- learn more about your favourite Piatkus authors

VISIT OUR WEBSITE AT: www.piatkus.co.uk

First published in Great Britain in 2005 by
Piatkus Books Ltd
5 Windmill Street, London W1T 2JA
email: info@piatkus.co.uk

This edition published in 2006

The moral right of the author has been asserted

A catalogue record for this book is available from the British Library

ISBN 0 7499 2756 9

Edited by Jan Cutler
Text design by Briony Chappell

This book has been printed on paper manufactured
with respect for the environment using wood from
managed sustainable resources

Data manipulation and page make-up by
Action Publishing Technology Ltd, Gloucester
Printed and bound in Great Britain by
Clays Ltd (St Ives plc)

For Adrian and James –
my personal overload solution

Contents

Acknowledgements   ix
Introduction   xi

Part One: The Problem   1

1 Are you overloaded, stressed – or both?   3
2 Warning! Overload can damage your health, your
  happiness and your relationships   16
3 The ten demons of overload   26
4 What doesn't work … and what does   39

Part Two: Short-term Fixes – Band-Aid for the Stressed Soul   49

5 The fork in the crossroads   51
6 Winning back time   64
7 Ten dramatic ways to reduce overload overnight   75
8 Practical help for stressed workers   86
9 The relationship MOT   100
10 Moving away from money madness:
   the financial detox   111
11 The four super stress-reducers   122

Part Three: The Solution to Banish Overload Forever

Part Three: The Solution to Banish Overload Forever | 135

12 Preparing for change | 137
13 Ego, self-esteem, the Self and the soul | 146
14 Now: the key to happiness | 158
15 Authenticity | 168
16 Downshift, simplify and slow down | 179
17 Death – the teacher of life | 192
18 The five extra secrets of a stress-free life | 202
19 Set yourself free | 213

Bibliography | 219
Resources | 222
Index | 229

Acknowledgements

This book is, in many ways, a team effort. I am deeply indebted to the many people who so generously contributed their time and wisdom to *The Overload Solution*: Sam Baker, Jules Bueno, Kat Byles, Jonny Chuter, Neil Crofts, Mark Curtis, Sarah Dening, Stephanie Driver, Michael Geary, Richard Jacobs, Richard Lawrence, Linda Lazarides, Brian and Sangeeta Mayne, Kate Offord, Will Parfitt, Jo Pickering, Tricia Sabine, Barry Schwartz, Jane Thurnell-Read, Deborah Tierney-Jones, Joy Toop, Sue Weston and Lisa Wynn.

In the past I have been helped enormously by another batch of wonderful people whose wise words also echo through *The Overload Solution*. They include Fiona Arrigo, Caroline Born, Robin Chandler, Christopher Connolly, Jane Duncan, Michael Edwards, Jo Ellen Grzyb, Robert Holden, Paul Z Jackson, Chris James, Karen Kingston, Richard Lanham, Susan Lever, Denise Linn, Sheila MacLeod, Ursula Markham, Jane Mayers, Ben Renshaw, Caroline Reynolds, Gabrielle Roth, Sarah Shurety, Kati St-Clair, Rolando Toro, Liz Williams, Nick Williams and Ann Marie Woodall.

I would like to thank Judy Piatkus and Gill Bailey of Piatkus Books for turning my mind to overload and giving me the opportunity to write this book, and to Helen Stanton, Jana Sommerlad and the rest of the team at Piatkus who transform a bunch of words into a 'real' book and make sure it gets out there to be read. A debt of gratitude to Jan Cutler for her meticulous care and wise suggestions. Love and thanks, as always, to my agent, Judith Chilcote, who introduced me to 'gratitude moments'. Thanks also to my staunch allies Camilla Collier, Cheryl Palin and Joanne Leonard, for sterling support.

Introduction

Do you wake up in the morning feeling just as exhausted as when you went to bed? Does the prospect of the day ahead fill you with untold dread? Are you juggling your life so fast and furiously that you can't even remember how many balls are supposed to be in the air? If life seems like one long struggle, you're not alone. Let's face facts: we're completely and utterly overloaded, and it's getting worse. Virtually every day I come across people who say, simply and sadly: 'I'm not coping.' I've written this book for them, and for you – because, fortunately, there *are* solutions and there *are* steps you can take to stop juggling and start living once again. I can't wave a magic wand and banish stress forever, but I *can* give you sure-fire strategies to kick overload back into place.

First of all, don't be too tough on yourself. Overload is not all your fault. The 21st century is an incredibly difficult place. Life is changing faster than anyone could have predicted, and our bodies, minds and emotions just aren't keeping up. You would need to be superhuman to keep pace with modern expectations. The idea of simply being 'stressed' would be almost appealing nowadays; instead, frightening numbers of us are suffering 'brownout' and burnout: serious conditions that lead to depression, anxiety and despair – in some cases mental or physical breakdown, even suicide. Psychologists are witnessing the onslaught of new and frightening phenomena, such as 'desk rage' where workers resort to stand-up rows with their colleagues because of work pressures. We're starting to hear about 'future shock syndrome', 'information fatigue syndrome' and 'data smog', as the information highway sends our minds into gridlock.

It's not just at work either. Cracks are appearing in our relationships, our families and in society as a whole. We feel ourselves failing as parents, as partners, as friends, as *people* – because, contrary to what we've been told by society and the media, we simply *can't* have it all. We've been sold a pup. Yet still we underplay overload and we deride people who cannot cope with it. Our inability to cope is seen as some kind of failing – the ultimate 21st-century sin. So we soldier on, driven by the ancient belief that life is tough and you have just got to grit your teeth and deal with it. Sadly, but predictably, we don't all rise to the challenge and triumph. Most of us feel inadequate and guilty because we imagine we're the only ones who feel this way. Yet the truth is, we're all facing much the same dilemmas – it's just that few of us will openly admit them. We're stifling our fears, our anxieties, our anger and our misery – and so the problem grows.

A recent survey found that more than 75 per cent of Americans alone feel they're not coping with overload. That's three out of every four people. In the UK, it's estimated that up to 90 per cent of all visits to GPs are the result of the effects of stress. Just pause a moment and take in the enormity of that. Next time you feel you're the only one who's not sailing through life, remember those figures.

I'm not immune. I'm as overloaded as many of you. I have to juggle a heavy workload (I write features and books – and often everyone wants them all at the same time) with the demands of a young child. My husband is self-employed as well and we don't have childcare, so sometimes our diary juggling would be hilarious if it all wasn't so frustrating. There are some weeks when we barely see one another, despite sleeping in the same bed. Add in elderly parents at opposite ends of the country and the fact that we live nearly an hour from the nearest large town. Do I feel the strain? Does the sun rise and set? Do rivers run to the sea? Yes, I am often overloaded, and no, I don't always cope.

So why should you trust me, and this book? Because I know the problems you have – they're my problems, too. Rest assured I'm not sitting in the lotus position preaching peace and lentils (more likely I'm typing with one hand while fixing a Lego dinosaur with the other).

Whereas I am often overloaded, I *have* learnt how to keep the demands of my life pretty much under control. Also, I do not suffer hugely from stress (I'll show you later why keeping stress under wraps is so vital). I grew up in a household where yoga and meditation were as much a part of daily life as breakfast. I learnt the art of good breathing, healthy food and creative visualisation at my mother's knee. By my teens, I was using homeopathy, herbs, aromatherapy, Bach flower remedies and healing on my (often bemused) friends. Later, when I grew up and became a journalist, I spent 15 years picking the brains of literally hundreds of experts in the fields of natural health, psychology and spirituality. All have been inspiring, and many have become good friends. I have learnt – by trial and error – what works and what is a waste of time (and what is often an expensive waste of time). Truly, I do walk my talk and I have found answers that work for me. However, we're all different and so, for this book, I asked many other people for their top strategies for beating overload. *The Overload Solution* truly is different. It's not one person's rose-tinted vision of a stress-free future. It's the amalgamated wisdom and common sense of many, many people: experts in stress relief, psychology, medita-tion, natural therapies and ancient philosophies.

You're not stupid. You know you're overloaded and, ten to one, you have tried ways of dealing with it. Unfortunately, when we're overloaded, we often aren't in a position to make the best decisions. It's all too easy to turn on the TV, to drown our sorrows in alcohol and gorge our bodies with 'comfort' food. I'll show you why these 'coping' strategies actually increase our overload. Equally, many of us have been papering the cracks, fondly imagining that we have found wonderful new ways to manage our lives and increase our personal sense of well-being. We have trusted in the flurry of New Age gurus who promised us the world. But now reality is setting in. We're realising that, sadly, the odd yoga class and a macrobiotic sandwich at lunchtime isn't going to save us from the sheer hell of chronic stress; thumbing through yet another self-help book on the way to work won't give us the lives we feel we should have.

There are not any easy answers and I'm not going to patronise you by suggesting you light another candle or take up watercolour painting as an instant solution to stress. Equally, I'm not going to present a blueprint for global reform – because that is unrealistic. It would be tempting to say, 'Hey, pack up work and head for the hills' but few of us can do that. I will, however, offer an honest appraisal of where we are now and then look at strategies that can help us readjust to this tough new world. I'm also going to offer practical, down-to-earth suggestions for shifting the way you think and act.

Chronic stress is now a global epidemic, linked to the six leading causes of death: heart disease, cancer, lung ailments, accidents, cirrhosis of the liver and suicide. Chronic stress is the grinding stress that wears people away day after day, year after year. It is, says the American Psychological Association, the kind of stress that 'destroys bodies, minds and lives. It wreaks havoc through long-term attrition. Chronic stress comes when a person never sees a way out of a miserable situation. It's the stress of unrelenting demands and pressures for seemingly interminable periods of time.' The worst aspect of chronic stress and overload is that we get used to it. We get so used to running on that treadmill, we forget it's there.

I'm a pragmatist, and I'd like to make it quite clear that I don't offer the promise of a stress-free life. I have no slick, glib answer to overload. There is no 'five-minute solution', no ten-step programme to a life of simplicity and ease. However, there *are* common-sense answers to many of the problems of overload, and these will, hopefully, help a lot of you. There are also some deeper, more metaphysical questions that, to my mind, need addressing in our frenetic society. Some of these may be unpalatable. Some you may dismiss out of hand as unworkable. Everybody is different and everyone needs to make their own decisions about how they live their lives. So, I have divided this book into three major sections. The first looks at 'the problem' of overload. Before you can attempt to solve a problem, you need to be able to identify it and look it straight in the face. Part One investigates the way our world has changed and continues to change (often so fast we don't see it move). We'll take a blunt look at the victims of overload – how our families, our social lives, our health and even our spirituality take body blows when our lives spiral out of control. Some of the causes of overload are obvious; others may come as quite a surprise. I'll also look at what *doesn't* work. We have a burgeoning self-help industry, a feeding frenzy of New Age consumerism. Ancient wisdom (which, in itself has much to say on overload and how to avoid it) has been plundered and diluted into often meaningless mumbo-jumbo and snake oil.

In Part Two I'll show you down-to-earth, pragmatic ways of reframing the problem. This section offers practical help for overloaded workers, suggestions for how to save your relationships from the ravages of overload. It suggests financial detox tips so that you can move away from money madness. I'll give you a plan for beating overload that really will make a huge difference – if you dare to follow it!

Finally, Part Three offers the potential for real change, a seismic shift in the way you perceive your life, the way you relate to the world around you. I'm not going to suggest you run away from overload. Living the hermit life is not a real option for most people. There simply isn't space for all of us to start small-holdings in the country and, let me assure you (as someone who lives in the heart of the country) there is just as much stress and overload out here as in the city. We can't turn back the clock either and become born-again peasants in homespun. The 21st century is calling for a new kind of person. Not a super-person, not the 'do-it-all, have-it-all' hero or heroine we thought we were seeking in the 1980s and 1990s, but rather the kind of person who knows almost exactly who he or she is. This new breed of person will have the self-knowledge to be able to sift the necessary from the unnecessary, to make tough decisions, to face unpalatable truths. They learn what is important and what matters, and jettison the rest. They find a deep sense of inner worth and peace simply being who they are rather than whom society demands they should be. You could be one of them.

Throughout the book there are questions to ask yourself and exercises to try. I hope that there will be many that resonate and work for you. You may notice that I often repeat questions, in slightly different ways. It's not a mistake or sloppy editing – it's because the psyche often needs to be nudged several times before it's willing to shift. Sometimes a slightly different way of saying something, or saying the same thing at a different time, will get through.

It's a tough world out there and we all have tough choices to make. But the good news is that we *do* have choices. You can choose, right now, to start getting a handle on overload. You can get stress under control – if *I* can crack it I promise you can, too.

Part One

The Problem

Chapter 1

Are you overloaded, stressed – or both?

Stress? Overload? Aren't they one and the same thing? Although the two are inextricably linked, they *are* different. If we want to take back control over our lives, we need to know our enemies. You probably think you know all there is to know about stress and overload – after all, you're living and breathing them every single day. But it can be useful to untangle the two, to understand what they are, and why they have become so overwhelmingly powerful in modern life.

Stress: our safety response

I'm not going to suggest you have no stress in your life. Short surges of stress hormones are useful: they make you smart and they make you fast. So let's not demonise stress. It's actually a totally natural and even essential process. Our prehistoric ancestors lived tough, often violent, lives. The stress mechanism was often a lifesaver and can still be as dramatic today. Under severe stress, we can do incredible things. Think about the tales of ordinary people who miraculously lift cars to free a trapped child. Think of the way time seems to slow down (allowing you to make the appropriate reaction) when you're in a dangerous situation. I remember having a tyre blow-out doing 80mph on an American highway. For a moment I saw red (literally) and then time seemed to slow right down. I told my passengers to keep calm, and slowly, so slowly (or so I thought) I pulled across three lanes of traffic to the central reservation and came to a halt. It was only when I got out of the car and saw the sharp-angled skid marks that I realised the whole incident had taken seconds.

The stress response (the classic 'fight or flight') comprises an incredibly complex series of reactions. It affects virtually every part of the body. In the past it would have been triggered by the primitive need to fight or run for your life. Today, it can be triggered by opening a huge tax demand, or getting ready for a tricky meeting. In other words, fight or flight isn't appropriate now. Let's take a look at what happens when your brain perceives a threat or challenge – why it was originally a useful response and how it can backfire nowadays.

How your body reacts to stress

Body system	What it does	Why it used to work	Why it causes problems now
Hypothalamus ('master gland' of brain)	Releases key chemicals to trigger stress response. Also releases endorphins	Endorphins are natural painkillers, allowing you to carry on running or fighting even if injured	Constant stress interferes with endorphin production, resulting in low mood, depression and anxiety

Body system	What it does	Why it used to work	Why it causes problems now
Adrenal glands	Release stress hormones such as cortisol, adrenalin and noradrenalin	Promote changes in the brain, heartbeat and metabolism, preparing the body for fight or flight	Build-up of these hormones reduces immune function, increases blood pressure and can lead to gut problems
Thyroid	Secretes hormones to speed up metabolism	Gives extra energy and alertness	Leads to anxiety, insomnia and nervous exhaustion
Digestive system	Shuts down	Blood is diverted to muscles for speed and strength	Abdominal cramps, nausea, bloating, diarrhoea, IBS (irritable bowel syndrome)
Heart	Beats faster	Pumps more blood to muscles and lungs	Can lead to high blood pressure and anxiety
Liver	Cholesterol released into the blood	Cholesterol takes over as a fuel when blood sugar is used up	Unused cholesterol sticks to the walls of blood vessels, leading to heart disease and stroke

Body system	What it does	Why it used to work	Why it causes problems now
Lungs	Breathing becomes faster	Supplies extra oxygen needed for increased blood flow	Can lead to hyperventilation, anxiety. Lung damage likely if you smoke while stressed
Skin	Sweating increases	Cools down skin when fighting or running	Sweaty, clammy feeling
Senses	Become more alert and sensitive	More able to detect threat and react swiftly	Edginess, jumpiness, nerviness
Mind	Sharpens. Cortisol and adrenalin enhance memory	Thinks up swift solutions; stores and retrieves useful information for future attacks	Constant arousal leads to confusion, exhaustion, anxiety, depression
Immune system	On red alert	Mobilises tissues in advance warning of wound or infection	Constant alert leads to depressed immune function, colds, infections, openness to auto-immune disease
Muscles	Tense. Releasing lactic acid into the bloodstream	On stand-by for action	Chronic tension, muscular pain, headache, anxiety, fear

This series of reactions happens incredibly swiftly and totally unconsciously. However, as you can see, when it comes on unnecessarily or lasts for more than a short time, its effects can be potentially damaging.

Stress makes us successful – and unhappy

Some researchers think that stress is actually a 'coping mechanism' for the demands of life. Highly successful people with high incomes tend to have more of the stress hormone cortisol in their bodies than others. Of course it could simply be that they have more stress in their lives. But some researchers believe it's the high stress hormones that give them the edge – that make them successful. Evolutionary psychologist Robert Wright, author of *The Moral Animal*, actually believes that we are not built to be happy, but to be merely 'effective'. He asserts that our very DNA is coded for discontentment, because in our past, discontent (and the stress it causes) was a survival strategy, pushing us to achieve and evolve.

Stress may have pushed us to invent the wheel; it may have hauled us out of the Dark Ages, but it's left us with a modern-day problem. We still suffer stress but we no longer know how to turn it off. For our prehistoric ancestors, stress came in short, sharp bursts. When our ancestors, the hunter-gatherers on the African plains, were not hunting, they would relax – completely – allowing their stress hormones to return to resting levels. Surviving hunter-gatherer tribes spend a small fraction of their time 'working' – most of the time they will sit around or snooze.

In overload situations, there is no opportunity for the letdown part of the cycle – the hormones pile up and simply don't disperse. Our body remains in a permanent twilight state of red alert, putting organs and body systems under strain.

Many researchers believe our old definitions of stress are no longer adequate. Professor Bruce McEwen, neuroendocrinologist, stress researcher and author of *The End of Stress as We Know it*, uses the phrase 'allostatic overload' for our inability to shut down from the stress response, and return to stability. He says:

> We need a new and more wide-ranging definition of stress to describe what happens to the body in the modern age. Today, many things build up over time and throw the stress response off-kilter: sleep loss, overwork, lack of social support, inadequate exercise, depression. When this happens we go into allostatic overload.

So what is overload?

Overload, as opposed to stress, is the cold, stark reality of having too much on your plate, of having to juggle too many balls, of having a load that is way too heavy for one person to carry – hence *over*load. It comes when you exceed your limits; when you are physically, emotionally and psychologically living on a knife-edge all the time, when you cannot take any more. You are pushed to the point where there is no margin in your life, no spaces around the edges for the things that really matter. You become time-poor, racing from task to task or trying desperately to multitask. Overload happens when you have too many demands pressing on you at the same time. You are overdrawn – not just at the bank but also at work, at home, everywhere.

It's a state that many of us take for granted as our lot. Time and time again, when I ask people about their experience of overload, they say, with a resigned shrug, 'Well, what choice is there?' Society demands overload, society approves of overload. The busier and more stressed you are, the more important you are seen to be.

The past 50 years have seen extraordinary growth and

progress. When I was a child there were no computers, no faxes, no mobile (cell) phones, no Internet, no CDs, no video games, no DVDs. Few people I knew had cars (and second cars were unheard of). People (generally men) tended to stick in one job for life. Change was pretty slow, almost imperceptible. I was the first person in my family to go to university, the first woman to have a career.

Progress is a double-edged sword, and while it has given us so much, it has also taken away a great deal, too – generally in terms of our peace of mind, our relationships and our sense of soul. As the world has opened up, we have come to expect more and more – both of the world, and of ourselves. We have been told that we can have it all, do it all, be whatever we want to be, have whatever we want to have – and we have believed it. We have come to assume that we are super-beings, that there are virtually no limits to what we can do. Whereas in the past, people generally had one major role – breadwinner or parent – now we habitually combine the two and, in addition, try to squeeze all those other roles – friend, child, grandchild, partner – into the interstices. We have become so used to pushing ourselves that we have lost any sense of balance.

Not only are we doing more but we're also doing it faster. It's as if we are on a nightmare carousel ride with a demonic force spinning us round and round, faster and faster until we become so dizzy we are in danger of falling off. Falling off, indeed, is what happens if we don't pay attention to the warning signs of overload. Burnout. Collapse. Breakdown. Chronic ill health. 'But it won't happen to me,' I can almost hear you say. Won't it?

How you become overloaded

Overload creeps up on you unawares. You start by taking on just one more duty, one more role and, before you know it, your diary is full, your in-tray bulging, your commitments overwhelming. At first you might be fine, you might even relish the sheer aliveness of living in the fast lane. You're firing on all cylinders and it feels great to be living on the edge. Then the headaches might start. Or the heartburn. You find yourself reaching more often for the indigestion tablets, the painkillers. You find it harder to get to sleep at night, so you pop the odd sleeping pill and that works a treat. Except that pretty soon the sleeping pills don't work so well and you have to take more. So you feel groggy in the morning and a skinny latte just doesn't do it any more; you need a double shot of espresso, and then maybe another to jolt you into the day. Every time your energy dips, you give yourself another shot (while your adrenal glands are crying out for mercy) or you boost your energy with a slab of chocolate or a biscuit (sending your blood-sugar levels hurtling up and plummeting down again like a rollercoaster).

By now your colleagues, family and friends are noticing that you are getting irritable, that you are on a permanent short fuse. Your sense of humour seems to have vanished and it's hard to get you to smile. Of course, they probably won't be seeing so much of you as you start working later and taking more work home to catch up. If anyone asks you for help, if your partner complains that he or she doesn't see you, if your child asks you to play, you find yourself feeling resentful and critical – don't they *know* you're busy? In fact, the whole world seems to be conspiring against you nowadays. Nobody drives fast enough any more and why the hell do they let some of these people have driving licences in the first place? You used to be a careful driver but now you find yourself overtaking more often, tailgating the slowcoaches, leaning on the horn and even flashing the finger at those inconsiderate idiots.

Next up, you find your immune system seems to have forgotten its purpose and you go down with every bug going. Of course you can't even think about taking time off – you just have to struggle on, dosing yourself with Beechams and Night

Nurse, NyQuil and Tylenol, and soldiering on.

While your body is letting you down, your mind isn't helping much either. You find it much tougher to make decisions than you used to. It's odd because you have never been an indecisive person. Your thoughts become ever more negative, ever more bleak and pessimistic. Are you reaching your targets? Is so-and-so after your job? Will you meet those huge mortgage payments? Anxiety levels rise and you find yourself becoming paranoid and jittery.

Then one day you wake up and it feels as if someone has turned all the colours of the world to grey. You are overwhelmed with fatigue, with a sense of 'how on earth can I go on?' All you want to do is turn over and hurl yourself back into oblivion. There seems no point to anything any more. Nothing is joyful. Nothing is good. Life has left you high and stranded. So you ask your doctor to fix it. She suggests you try counselling but you simply don't have time for weekly sessions and, besides, it's much easier to pop a Prozac.

This might continue for many years – humans are incredibly hardy. But meanwhile any genetic or environmental susceptibilities you have will start to combine with the stress to create any number of time bombs. If you have a predisposition to heart failure, stroke, cancer, IBS, colitis and so on, overload might be all it takes to tip your body into the disease. Left unchecked, overload and stress can exacerbate auto-immune disorders, such as multiple sclerosis or rheumatoid arthritis. They are believed to be a strong factor in chronic fatigue syndrome (CFS). Researchers have found that, contrary to previous doubt, stress *is* often a factor in miscarriage.

Of course, you might be immune. Just as a rare few people can smoke cigarettes all their lives and miraculously escape cancer, some people are more resilient to overload than others. But I wouldn't count on it. In fact, you might just be particularly susceptible. Clinical psychologist Elaine N Aron, author of *The*

11

Highly Sensitive Person, has identified a group she calls HSP ('highly sensitive people') who are more likely to wear down swiftly, who succumb far more easily to overload. Who are these people? Generally, creative and empathetic people – exactly those who are most likely to put themselves in positions of overload.

Overload affects everyone

Both genders and all ages are hit by overload. It is not picky. Initially I thought that overload was something that didn't really affect 20-somethings. I thought that maybe there was at least one decade in which you could simply enjoy life – free from the pressures of exams but not yet burdened by family, mortgage and conflicting demands. Wrong. Sam Baker, editor of *Cosmopolitan* magazine pointed out frightening statistics amongst this supposedly 'carefree' group. Nearly 60 per cent of 18–24 year olds feel stressed, with over 70 per cent stressed about money. A further 70-plus per cent feel that depression is a 'big issue' amongst their peers. US *Cosmopolitan* found its young readers were increasingly anxious about overload – they found technology 'a tether not a freedom'; they felt as if they were 'constantly under-performing and disappointing' and they worried that they were 'never able to shut down.' Remember: this is amongst the so-called 'freedom generation' who, for the most part, haven't even started trying to juggle work with having children and elderly dependants.

Are you suffering from overload?

Overload hits different people in different ways. However, most experts agree that there are certain common symptoms to show if someone is overloaded, or on the way to becoming overloaded.

Physical symptoms
- Over- or under-active digestive tract, indigestion, bowel upsets, IBS, constipation, piles, ulcers.
- Difficulties in sleeping – either unable to get to sleep or waking early.
- Bouts of what feels like jet lag – although you haven't been travelling.
- Chronic tiredness and exhaustion, even early in the day and after a good night's sleep.
- Increase in heart rate or blood pressure. Palpitations. Dizziness.
- Increased reliance on caffeine, alcohol, tobacco, drugs.
- Decreased interest in sex, possibly impotence.
- Headaches, migraine.
- Physical tension, muscle pain, backache, sciatica.
- Increased infections, colds and flu.
- Aggravation of chronic conditions such as eczema, asthma.

Mental symptoms
- Difficulties in concentrating; hearing but not fully grasping what you have heard or read.
- Forgetfulness.
- Recurring anxious thoughts.
- Lack of confidence in your ability to perform.
- Irritability, anger, a 'short fuse'.
- Lack of interest in things you used to find exciting or interesting.
- Impatience, intolerance.
- Mental fatigue – you will go for a tried-and-trusted approach rather than look for new solutions.
- Over-reaction to problems.
- Avoiding necessary but non-urgent tasks and relying on crisis management to get by.
- Depression.

- Lack of discrimination – inability to prioritise.
- Over-compensating behaviour – over-analysing, over-checking when strictly unnecessary.
- Reluctance to offer support.

Emotional symptoms

- Feeling discouraged or emotionally down without an obvious reason.
- Feeling guilty or sad about neglecting family, friends and your own real interests.
- Anger at your job, boss or colleagues, because you feel trapped.
- Anger and disappointment at your family because they don't appreciate what you are doing for them.
- Irritation at people who demand your time or attention.
- Ambivalent feelings about success – relief you carried it off but a curious disappointment, too.
- Feeling unable to give time or attention to other people's problems – and resentful that they try to put them on you.
- Rising sense of panic – of being unable to cope.
- Feeling of being trapped.
- Crying and out-of-character outbursts.
- Aggressive behaviour and sudden mood changes.

Feedback from others

- Complaints that you are ignoring people, not giving time to friends and family.
- Complaints that that you are leaving your partner with the entire job of looking after the family.
- Complaints that 'you love your job more than you love me'.
- Concerns that you aren't listening to work colleagues. That you aren't paying attention to colleagues' or staff's needs.
- Concern that the quality of your work is suffering.

Do you recognise yourself in any part of this? Remember that overload can creep up unawares so it's worth knowing the warning signs.

Stress v overload

While it's clear that stress does not equal overload, I will be suggesting ways to tackle stress. It's a bit of a chicken-and-egg situation. You're overloaded so you get stressed. Yet the more stressed you get the less able you are to cope with overload. There must be a rare handful of people who can juggle too many roles and work too many hours while staying as cool and calm as a cucumber – but I don't know any. *The Overload Solution* is for the huge majority of us who can't juggle or are fed up to the back teeth with juggling. It's a tough problem, but you *can* unravel it and claw back control.

Chapter 2

Warning! Overload can damage your health, your happiness and your relationships

You cannot do it all. You can do a lot, a heck of a lot, but all of it? No. Trying to do it all equals overload, and that leaves you exhausted, irritable and ragged around the edges. It also poses serious risks – physically, psychologically and emotionally – to your life. Don't be tempted to just muddle through – truly, the price is just too high.

When you are overloaded, living under chronic stress, the stress response we looked at in the last chapter eventually starts malfunctioning. You still produce the same hormones but your brain stops regulating them effectively. They might keep spiking unnecessarily or not shut down properly. Unfortunately, when this starts to happen, your hormones are no longer activating your immune system; they're suppressing it. You no longer enjoy the sharp thinking of the stress response because the nerve cells in your brain actually start to shrink. Chemical messengers that remain active for too long may damage the hippocampus in the brain, and it's hypothesised that this could be a triggering factor in depression. Meanwhile, nerve cells in the amygdala part of the brain (which mediates feeling) actually produce *more* dendrites (the antennae of the nerve cells) under repeated stress, increasing anxiety and fear.

In the last chapter we saw the huge array of ailments overload can cause. Naturopath Stephanie Driver says, 'Stress plays a role in the development of many serious chronic diseases. The main problem with chronic stress is that it permanently raises cortisol secretion. Chronically high cortisol levels lead to abdominal obesity, type 2 diabetes, blood-sugar problems, and general inflammation in the body.' Researchers have even found that overload plays a major role in the premature ageing of cells. Women with the highest levels of stress undergo the equivalent of ten years additional ageing, compared to women with the lowest stress. Bottom line? Chronic stress can take years off your life.

The depression and anxiety epidemics

For every person openly struggling with stress, there are probably several more who fall outside the official statistics because they are not 'officially' suffering from stress – they are depressed.

Depression

More than 2.9 million people in the UK alone are diagnosed as having depression. But that's just the tip of the iceberg. It's estimated that a staggering 75 per cent of those suffering from depression are neither recognised nor treated.

Of course, depression can be brought on by a host of purely physiological causes. However, very frequently, depression has a psychological cause, initiated by stress. A problem with work, relationships, money, health or sleep can tip us into depression. Put several of these together, as in overload, and it's no wonder many people endure the company of the black dog. I know all about depression: it's like trying to run a race with someone hanging on to your heels all the way. Add depression to your average overload and no wonder people are sinking.

Anxiety

Anxiety is also on the increase. A phenomenal 19 million Americans are believed to be affected by anxiety disorders. In the UK, one in ten people is likely to have an anxiety disorder. Left untreated, anxiety can mushroom and may lead to panic attacks, social anxiety disorder, obsessive-compulsive disorder (OCD) and phobias.

The National Institutes of Health in the US is so concerned about the numbers of people suffering from anxiety that they now even have a dedicated Center for the Neuroscience of Fear and Anxiety to study our increasing levels of anxiety.

Unfortunately, if we allow our fears and anxieties to run free, they will snowball. Studies of rats show that once a fear is learnt, chemical pathways form in the brain so that the next fear to come along is learnt even more quickly. Stress and phobias, if left unchecked, will pick up speed and increase exponentially, all on their own. We can actually 'learn' anxiety – and we're very good at it. Professor Bruce McEwen says, 'Anticipating impending confrontations, ruminating on endless "what ifs" and "if onlys" can send our stress hormones surging and have measurable effects on the cardiovascular and neuroendocrine systems. If we torture ourselves with worst-case scenarios, we can exhaust our bodies' stress response without even leaving home.' In Part Two we'll look at ways to stop anxiety spiralling out of control.

The emotional victims of overload

When we are overloaded, something has to give and so, often quite unconsciously, we cut back on certain areas of our lives. In our work and money-obsessed culture, it's rare that work will be the first to have its head laid on the block. So, for most people, there are five major victims of overload: relationships, children, family (and in a wider sense, community), creativity and spirituality. Let's take a look at each in turn.

Overload victim #1: relationships

More marriages now fail than survive. Most split even before the infamous seven-year itch has a chance to sharpen its fingernails. There are many reasons for this, but undoubtedly overwork and overavailability are obvious contenders. How many relationships try (and fail) to compete with the job? This is nothing new, of course; we all know the stereotype of the businessman (in the past it used to be just men) so wedded to his desk he could barely recognise his children. However, in the past, work ended for most people as they left the office, the factory or the shop. Now work comes home and even snuggles into bed with us in the shape of always-on mobiles or the laptop open on the bedside table.

It's ironic that in a world in which we have more communication devices than ever before, we are less able to talk. In fact, some experts believe that the Internet, texting and other digital technologies threaten relationships by making it easier to toy with other partners. Is it adultery if you have 'txtsex' or cybersex rather than physical sex? Is it OK if you hang out in chat rooms rather than meet up in physical bars? We can blur the lines between reality and fantasy, we can kid ourselves that because it's digital it doesn't count, but we still damage our relationships. Divorce Online (a UK divorce advice and information website) reports that half of all divorce petitions it processes involve Internet adultery and cybersex behaviour. A quarter of Europeans claim to have engaged in txtsex.

We now live in a culture where your choices do not have to be permanent: everything is throwaway, dispensable, subject to return or exchange. Why should relationships be any different? It's frightening to see how easily, almost thoughtlessly in many cases, we now change our life partners. Even if we do stay together, it's at a price. Exhausted women (and men) say they would rather lie in the arms of Morpheus, the Greek god of dreams, than those of their lover. We're too tired for sex, too tired even to argue most of the time. According to the Chartered Institute of Personnel and Development, over half of their partners said their sex life was suffering because the partner who was working long hours was too tired.

Do relationships suffer when you're overloaded? I rest my case.

Overload victim #2: children

A child can pick up a parent's anxiety and stress as if by telepathy. Two-thirds of children say they are worried about their parents, particularly about their stress and tiredness. In a warped reversal of roles, many children nowadays are (or feel) responsible for caring emotionally for their own mothers and fathers.

Around a half of working mothers say they would like to give up work if they could afford to, and stay at home to look after their children. But who *can* afford to? Some parents guiltily admit that work is even a refuge from an increasingly chaotic home-life. The UK government is keen to encourage parents (and in particular women) back to work at the earliest possible opportunity. But if parents return to work, who is left holding the baby? In most cases (given the lack of family support available) it is a stranger – a nanny or, more usually, a nursery. Studies show that a good nursery can be a positive experience for pre-schoolers, boosting cognitive and social skills, with the proviso that they don't start too young. It's a vital distinction. But who can afford to keep their child at home until the optimum age of three?

Once a child starts school you'd think the parental overload would cease to be quite so significant. Not so. Overloaded parents have no option but to send sick children to school when they should be tucked up in bed, or to plunge them into a crammed day of breakfast clubs, after-school clubs, extensive play-dates and out-of-school programmes to bridge the gap between the end of school and their departure to, or return from, work. In Japan it's gone further still: children are now routinely booked into 24-hour child-minding centres. It begs the question – why have children if you hardly ever see them?

A whole industry of pseudo-parenting has grown up whereby you can now pay people not only to look after your children but also to help them with their homework, prepare them for academic success, even plan their parties and fill their party bags. The average working parent apparently spends twice as long dealing with emails as playing with his or her children. Above all, we are raising a generation of children for whom hurrying is a normal and natural (and stressful) part of life. Relaxation, kicking around, doing nothing is almost unknown. A survey by Norwich Union Healthcare found 78 per cent of parents thought their children were under greater pressure than when they were growing up.

Caught between a rock and a hard place, it's a tough call for modern parents, but even tougher for our children.

Overload victim #3: family and community

In an overworked, overloaded culture, nobody has time to care. Some women are too overloaded even to *have* a family. A study by *Good Housekeeping* magazine showed that 61 per cent of women working full-time said their job had damaged their family life, and 25 per cent that they had delayed starting a family in the hope that things would get easier when they were further up the career ladder. At least 20 per cent of women trying to conceive are now over 40, and a 66-year-old woman was in the news recently for giving birth. Couples are asking fertility clinics to give them twins so that they can have 'instant families' – either to minimise disruption to their careers or because older mothers-to-be fear they may not be able to conceive more than once. It's a 'buy one, get one free' attitude that speaks volumes about our society.

As a child I remember frequent visits to relatives for tea, for lunch, or just to drop off a batch of biscuits or a cake. Now, most people find it tough to manage Sunday lunch as a family. Whereas families would meet up at social and religious functions – church, committees, coffee mornings – these have all been lost to our work culture.

Grandparents used to take an active role in the upbringing of children – now most grandparents are themselves either still working or, as more and more of us have our children later and later, too elderly and frail to be able to cope.

The ageing population

As our pensioner population grows (it's projected to increase by nearly a fifth between 2006 and 2021), 300,000 people in the UK alone become carers every year. Many (particularly women) are caught with the dual demands of looking after both young children and elderly parents – *and*, in many cases, working as well. Many more elderly people live lonely lives, coping alone or sitting in homes, waiting for the visits that nobody has time to make.

Having good connections with friends and relatives has been proven to help prevent overload yet, ironically and sadly, who manages the time for a social life? Friendships, particularly once one has a family, frequently fall into disrepair. According to a study by the Mental Health Foundation in the UK, nearly half the population say they have slimmed down their social life, seeing less of friends.

If we don't have time for family or friends, what hope for those looser yet still vital acquaintances and commitments? Who, nowadays, has time to volunteer? Organisations, such as the scouting movement, report that there is a chronic shortage of people willing to lead or help with groups. The Improvement and Development Agency for Local Government in the UK talks of a 'missing generation of twenty-five to forty-year olds'. Charities and churches have to rely on an increasingly ageing army of volunteers. Do we suffer because of this? I believe so. We miss out on the varied social fabric of our community and our world becomes less involved, less caring.

Overload victim #4: creativity

The people around us certainly suffer when we are overloaded. However, we suffer, too. Can you recall a time when you had pastimes, hobbies? When you used to do things for fun or for the 'sheer hell of it'? Bet you're hunting way back in time. According to a study by the Mental Health Foundation, nearly half of us have had to cut out our hobbies and entertainment due to the rapacious demands of work. Hobbies. It sounds an old-fashioned word nowadays and, who knows, may soon pass into the realms of myth. Who now has the time to do the crossword, to doodle, to stare out of the window? Erstwhile common pursuits, such as knitting, have now become the pastimes of the rich – supermodels and actresses wax lyrical about the joy of knitting. It's touted as a return to the 'simplicity' of life, yet, in reality, it's a status symbol. Only those who are wealthy have the leisure to spend quiet pensive hours clicking needles.

The human soul yearns to be creative and we are drawn to the quaint and curious. Yet how many of us spare the time to follow our dreams? Modern society approves only of improving pastimes, learning 'for a purpose' rather than learning for fun, or simply doing nothing much at all. We have lost the gentle art of wasting time.

Overload victim #5: spirituality

I'm not religious in the rigid sense but I deeply lament the passing of the Sabbath. One day a week without shopping, working, consuming – is that too much to ask? Evidently so. There was always a different energy about Sunday in the past. The roads were quieter, the air somehow stiller. Even if we didn't always go to church, we did things together as a family – we had a proper lunch, we played games, we talked.

Should we be concerned that overload is taking away our sense of spirit? I think so. The famous psychologist C G Jung said, 'The lack of meaning in life is a soul-sickness whose full extent and full import our age has not as yet begun to comprehend.' Where do we find meaning in our lives? On a superficial level we find it in our work and our persona, the face we present to the outside world. But on a deep, soul level we find it by turning inwards, away from the world, in the quiet, thoughtful, soulful moments that are such anathema to overload.

Nowadays we lament the lack of 'me time' and it sounds selfish. But time alone, time quiet is important, nay vital, to the soul and is a staunch ally in beating overload. Musing time, meditative time, has disappeared in a puff of smoke. Magazines advise you to 'take time to pamper yourself' – by having a bath. It's a sad indictment of modern life that the only time you can have time to yourself is by locking yourself in the bathroom, the only way you can connect with spirit is to light an aromatherapy candle.

On a purely physical level one should seek the spiritual. Research shows clearly that it is healthy to have a faith, to pray, to meditate, to muse. When we don't have time for spirituality, when we push aside the quiet pleas of our souls, we are diminished as human beings, we only half-live.

Chapter 3
The ten demons of overload

We've seen what can happen when we're overloaded, but what causes the problem? If you're overloaded, you have probably never even had the chance to think about it. It's just, well, *everything* about your life. But there are actually ten distinct factors that mass together to create tension, anxiety, stress, overload. I call them the Ten Demons of Overload because they suck away (rather like J K Rowling's Dementors) all joy and peace and contentment. These 'demons' or, if you'd rather be less dramatic, *factors*, are all part of everyday life. In spelling them out, the purpose is not to depress you, but to start a process of change. In the war against overload, we need to know what we're fighting. The ancient magicians used to believe that in order to gain power over a demon you needed to know its name. So let's name and shame our overload demons.

Demon 1: information

Gathering information used to be a slow, mindful process. You would go to a library and sift through the pages of books and journals, or pick up the telephone and talk to a real live person.

We used to go in search of information. Now a veritable tsunami of information comes seeking us – and threatens to overwhelm us.

We have had more information in the past 30 years than in all the previous 5,000 years combined. I expect you have heard the incredible statistic that the Sunday edition of the *New York Times* carries more information than the average 19th-century person would access in his or her entire life. The Internet is doubling in content every hundred days (at the time of writing) while 90 per cent of all the scientists who have ever lived are alive today – each dishing out more and more and more information. Go away from your desk for an hour and you'll come back to a rash of emails. Dare to go away for a week or two and your inbox will be overflowing.

Gone are the days when you would update your skills every few years. Now it is quite impossible to stay on top of the new information, the new research, the new technologies, the new techniques.

Information Fatigue Syndrome

Psychologist David Lewis proposed the term 'Information Fatigue Syndrome' (IFS) for the increased tension and ill health caused by widespread 'information overload'. Symptoms include poor decision-making, anxiety, difficulties in memorising and remembering, and reduced attention span. IFS can lead to increased cardiovascular stress (due to a rise in blood pressure), confusion and frustration, impaired judgement and even weakened vision.

It's not even as if we're getting good information. As a result, instead of becoming more certain about the truth, we become more insecure, more anxious. Surveys repeatedly find that an

Internet search will usually involve sorting through a deluge of dross to find just one pearl. This overabundance of poor-quality information is so prevalent it even has its own name: 'data smog'. David Shenk, who coined the phrase, reports that in the average office 60 per cent of each person's time is spent processing documents, and the typical business manager is said to read one million words per week.

According to Mark Curtis, digital information expert and author of *Distraction*, approximately 40 per cent of all email on the Internet is spam, and now it's hitting mobiles, too. Curtis reports that the cost of spam (chiefly in lost time) has been estimated as £13.4 billion a year for US and European businesses.

Demon 2: time

Increasing numbers of us are 'cash rich/time poor'. We 'speed-date', we eat on the run, we have face-lifts in our lunch-hour, we text instead of meeting up. Our very vocabulary mirrors our preoccupation – we have fast food, a rush hour, express trains, we live life in the fast lane. The protestant work ethic has become the overwork ethic as more and more of us work longer and longer hours. The old idea of a 'job for life' is a distant memory in the UK and America – you are only as good as your last day, your last hour. Even if you remain on top form, someone younger and cheaper may still replace you. Nearly two-thirds of junior and middle managers in the UK feel insecure. There is no such thing as job security, so it's no wonder we all work our socks off like there's no tomorrow – because tomorrow might be the day we get our cards.

Overworking
Nearly 46 per cent of men and 32 per cent of women work more hours than their contracts stipulate. Many simply work

until it is done, often from early in the morning until late at night. Only 44 per cent of British workers take all the holiday to which they are entitled. The average lunch 'hour' is now under half an hour and often involves grabbing a sandwich to eat at one's desk. The concept of tea breaks is a distant myth. Over half of British workers say they are too busy even to go to the loo.

Many of us are suffering the side effects of lack of sleep as we trim the only part of the day left – our hours in bed. Now a new drug, Provigil, offers the possibility of functioning for 48 hours without sleep. Some biochemists believe it will become possible to manage on as little as two to three hours of sleep per night.

Time is out of hand and yet, bizarrely, instead of admitting we are unfairly overloaded, we blame ourselves. We tell ourselves we aren't coping; that we have poor 'time-management skills' and therefore we are incompetent. It's 'our fault'.

Perhaps the most telling statistic of all is that a quarter of us would love to quit our jobs.

Demon 3: availability

Once upon a time the only people 'on call' at all hours were the emergency services (and they had rotas). Now we live in 24/365 time – always on call, never able to switch off. It's not just work either – with email, texting, mobiles and BlackBerries the social can reach into the workplace just as work can reach into home and social life. There are no longer any boundaries.

As the *Wall Street Journal* wryly commented on the cult of accessibility, 'The good news is, you're always connected to the office. The bad news is, you're always connected to the office.' It's affecting children, too. A study conducted by the University of Leuven in Belgium, published in the *Journal of Sleep*

Research, claims that the noise of text messages arriving in the middle of the night was affecting the sleep quality of almost half of all 16 year olds.

If you're always available, always 'on', you're not in control of your life – and lack of control is a key factor in determining what makes stress become dangerous. The stress caused by lack of, or low, control in the work environment, can lead to an increased risk of coronary heart disease. A Finnish study found that people who faced a combination of high demands at work, but poor control over their job, had double the risk of death from heart disease.

The other part of the availability syndrome is 'presenteeism' – where we work beyond the call of duty, beyond even efficiency, just to prove that we are there, that we're working as hard, if not harder than anyone else. It's a badge of pride to be the first one in and the last one out. We even go to work when we're ill. Professor Michael Marmot, epidemiologist, of University College London, warns that people doing this 'could be hastening their own deaths. The stress prompted by going to work when ill is an independent factor when calculating the risk to an employee's health through coronary heart disease.'

Demon 4: status

As a society we have never lived with such riches. Yet we never feel we have enough, we never feel we are good enough. We look at what the people around us have, and have achieved, and feel anxious and resentful, particularly if these achievements belong to people we consider our peers. It comes down to that old maxim – it's better to be a big fish in a small pond than a small fish in a big pond. Even better, in fact, to be an average-sized fish in a pond full of other average-sized fish. 'There are few successes more unendurable than those of our close friends,' says Alain de Botton, author of *Status Anxiety*. Unpalatable but true.

In his intriguing book, *The Paradox of Choice*, Professor Barry Schwartz says that concern for status has 'exploded into a kind of arms race of exquisiteness. The only way to be the best is to have the best ... "Good enough" is never good enough; only the best ... will do.' It's tough enough out there trying to earn sufficiently and juggle the demands of work and family without having to worry that you're not cutting the mustard with your peers, without having to feel you must always have the right things, the *best* things.

As if that weren't bad enough, we are fed a constant dose of celebrity envy via the media. We are not only desperate to keep up with the Joneses but we are also told we should aspire to the trimmings and trappings of celebrities – those new gods and goddesses of our time. It's a feeding frenzy with every magazine and paper having its own 'celeb watch' analysing the clothes, figures, relationships of people who are – well, what? Models, actors, television presenters, footballers. Perfectly nice people, I'm sure, many of whom are totally perplexed by the adoration. We compare ourselves to these people and find ourselves lacking.

Demon 5: choice

We live in a world packed with so much opportunity, it hurts; so much choice, it creates confusion. It ranges from the small choices (which shoes, which shade of off-white paint, which size boob job?) to the large issues (should I change my job, should I have children, should I move to a better place?).

Even the simplest choices have become difficult. Faced with 250 types of toothpaste, which should you pick? Shopping used to be generic: we went to the grocery store and asked for 'carrots' or 'baked beans' or 'pasta'. Now each item in the shopping trolley involves decisions: organic, non-organic, peeled, chopped, diced, baby; low-fat, low-sugar, no-sugar, in chilli, with sausages and so on. Don't even let's go into pasta or we'll still be there ten pages later. Futurologist Alvin Toffler, author of the seminal book *Future Shock*, says, 'We are, in fact, racing towards "overchoice".' As a society, we crave choice but it comes at a price, and that price is our psychic well-being. Too much choice is, quite simply, exhausting. When there is so much, nothing is special. More worryingly, when you have so many choices, how can you ever be sure you have made the right decision? Psychologists now talk about 'anticipated regret' appearing even before the purchase is made. How will you feel if you buy these shoes only to find a better pair in the next store?

Of course, the flipside is not taking decisions at all. The Future Foundation, a group of trend forecasters, say that around five per cent of women in their thirties who plan to have children, never will. Brian Mayne, co-author of *Life Mapping*, says, 'You would think choice to be a good thing. But now more people are needing to make more life-changing choices, about their work, about their family, about their own beliefs, than ever before.'

Some modern choices are almost impossible to call. Should you turn off the life-support system? Should you vaccinate your child with the MMR? Doctors, terrified of malpractice suits, now prefer to let their patients take decisions. One tale tells of an emergency surgeon in the US actually turning to the parents of a sick child and saying, 'Do you want me to intubate?' No doubt about it, too much choice and too tough choices overload us.

Demon 6: perfection

Our expectations rise by the minute and a huge number of us lurch from day to day in a never-ending cycle of desire, hope, striving, achievement, disappointment and regret. We may live in a nice enough house, but should we trade up? Might there be a better job around the corner? Why have an OK body when you could have a perfect one? Why settle for a decent enough partner when there could be someone way better out there if you only looked. Stressful? You bet.

Some of us are more vulnerable to the perfection trap than others – we (and I include myself purposefully here) are what psychologists call 'maximisers'. Maximisers seek and accept only the best – it's the fancy new term for what we used to call perfectionists. Maximisers need to feel sure that every decision, every purchase is the best that could be made. It's a hard call. It's one thing to choose between good and bad, but when the choice is between good and better, or better and best, you're in a real overload situation.

....

The rise of cosmetic surgery

Perfection goads us into having more and more cosmetic surgery. Nine out of ten Britons want to change something about their appearance, a quarter dream of a 'dramatic overhaul'. Last year the number of operations increased by a phenomenal 52 per cent. It's not just tummy tucks and facelifts either. Incredibly, people now even tinker with their belly buttons to get the perfect shape, and have the fat 'pad' over their knees dissolved.

....

Homes magazines and hoards of television programmes exhort us to improve our homes, changing our decor as frequently as we shift our wardrobe. 'The New Season's Colours' scream the headlines from the glossy magazines, the *Vogues* of the interiors world. Oh, OK, quick, let's repaint the whole house in taupe or emerald or whatever. Tear out the fitted kitchen; it's so passé. Up with the carpet and lay bamboo or leather or whatever this season demands. Oh, get real.

We have become a greedy society, always wanting more, always expecting more. It's not good enough to have one, or even two parts of our lives that work well – we expect it all to be incredible. We beat ourselves into a frazzle trying to have it all, to have it best and to have it quicker. Young people nowadays are being thrown into depression when they discover that that perfect media job doesn't drop into their laps the way they had expected. The 'have it all' generation are discovering that you can dream, you can try, but life isn't always fair and is often a gamble.

Nowadays we don't ever say, 'that's enough. I'm satisfied.' We push ourselves relentlessly to fulfil our expectations. We constantly compare our lives with the images of perfection we see in the media – and of course we fall short. So we change jobs, we ditch our partners, we cut-and-paste our bodies, we strip our walls in the desperate hope that this time we'll get it right. Of course, it never lasts.

Demon 7: change

Change is exciting, intoxicating and addictive. But all the factors that create stress involve change: marriage, divorce, moving house, illness, shifting jobs, even going on holiday.

Alvin Toffler suggested, back in the 1970s, that the huge acceleration of change in our world and its psychological effects would lead to a set of severe physical and mental disturbances that he dubbed 'future shock syndrome'. 'Change is the process by which the future invades our lives,' said Toffler, 'future shock is the shattering stress and disorientation that we induce in individuals by subjecting them to too much change in too short a time.'

He foresaw the most common result would be anxiety, showing itself in irrational fears. He was right. We are consumed with anxiety about what we perceive to be an ever more dangerous world *out there*. Our list of fears spreads ever farther and farther, and creates an overload of fear, worry and stress. Once again, we can lay much of the blame on the media. News focuses on the frightening and the bizarre, its currency is disaster and death and it thrives on fear and conflict. So it's not surprising that news picks up on the bad and, on the whole, ignores the good. Unfortunately, our brains aren't good at picking up on what is *not* stated. We latch on to the one train or plane that crashed and conveniently forget the many millions that didn't. As humans we have a frightening capacity for empathy; we hear about a tragedy and can immediately feel it as if it were our own. Empathy is a good quality; it makes us uniquely human – yet it doesn't serve us well in a society that focuses on the bad, rather than the good. Awful things *do* happen, they always have. Our mistake is to think that they are getting worse. Statistics prove that, actually, it's simply not true. We worry that the economy will collapse, that natural resources will run out, that genetic engineering will launch a bio-horror, that terrorism will wreck Western society. In the past, we would have worried only about direct local concerns – far more manageable. As Joseph LeDoux, a stress researcher at New York University says:

> People of the past were stressed by things they encountered personally, that were in the limited field of individual vision. Now everybody knows about everything going wrong all over the world, and about every conjectured threat. The inventory of things that sound like you need to be worried about has risen dramatically.

Demon 8: money

Money stress has always been with us. Yet now we have found ever more inventive ways of creating money stress. In the UK, as house prices soared, some lenders offered up to six times people's salaries and 50- or 100-year mortgages to enable people to buy a home.

Credit cards

Record numbers of people are being made bankrupt because they are falling behind on their credit-card bills. The UK's national credit-card debt is nearly £60 billion. In America, the picture is the same with credit-card debt doubling every five years.

On both sides of the Atlantic we are also using our credit cards to 'spave' money. Spaving means you spend with the (misguided) notion that you are saving money. It's the case of the £700 television reduced to £500, so you 'spave' £200. Illogical overloaded thinking at its most inventive.

If that isn't daft enough, how about home-equity lines of credit that can be accessed in seconds using ATM cards? You want that new SUV? Put it against your home. Remember that 'credit' in fact equals 'debt' and that debt brings mental and physical problems so severe that some doctors' surgeries have even started holding debt clinics to combat the associated health problems.

Demon 9: stuff

We are getting into debt purely because we want more and more stuff. Americans spend more on jewellery and watches than they do on higher education. America has twice as many shopping centres as it does high schools. Before the rest of us get smug, the 'need and greed' culture is not just an American phenomenon. There is a blurring of want and need throughout Western culture. Jonathan Chuter, corporate consultant and healer says:

Our own material expectations have grown, fuelled by what others have and we don't – people associate quality of life with more and more material goods. Most households now have two wage earners, in order to pay for the 'improved lifestyle' that all the media tell us we should be having. Second homes, holidays in distant places, two (sometimes three) cars including the obligatory 4×4, wide-screen TVs, video phones, the list is endless.

The term for our relentless dysfunctional pursuit of money is 'affluenza'. Affluenza is where overload, status, debt and anxiety join up in the frenzied pursuit of more and yet more. It is where we find ourselves in the bind of having to work ever harder in order to be able to afford more stuff. I also love the expression 'house bloat', which refers to the building of ever more gargantuan homes, cuckoos on a block of average-sized houses. The *Wall Street Journal* quoted a leading builder of bloated homes, who bragged, 'We sell what nobody needs.'

What do you do with your bloated house? Fill it with loads of stuff of course. We seek relief from our stresses and strains by shopping, by acquiring stuff. Then we worry whether we have the right stuff, good enough stuff, perfect stuff. Then we even worry that we have too much stuff and spend a further fortune on a professional declutterer to come and tell us what to get rid of. Or we call in a feng shui expert to help us move our stuff around in the hopes of attracting more wealth so, presumably, we can buy more stuff. Is that sane?

Demon 10: poor lifestyle

Researchers also warn that our modern lifestyle choices – our diet, exercise and sleep patterns – are having a deleterious effect on our stress levels. Studies have shown that people who are overweight or eat high-fat diets produce excessive levels of cortisol, leading, once again, to an increase in the stress response. Given that our nations are getting fatter and fatter on our fast-food diet, it seems likely that our stress levels will expand on a par with our waistlines. A study by the London Metropolitan University found that the average waist of children aged 11–16 has increased by 6 centimetres (2½ inches) in the past ten years, whereas the British Heart Foundation warn that over 20 per cent of girls aged two to 15 are overweight. Boys fare slightly better but 16 per cent are still overweight.

While we all know the benefits of regular exercise, we tend to shut our ears, preferring to grab a TV dinner and slob out in front of the television. We are committing what you could call 'sofa suicide', allowing our arteries to clog and our muscles to waste.

It's a sly trick of nature, but stress causes insomnia and insomnia certainly causes stress, creating a vicious nightmare circle of misery. As the *Sleep SOS Report* from the UK Sleep Alliance says:

> At a time when the 24/7 attitude dominates western culture and time asleep is viewed as wasted time, many consider that a need for sleep indicates laziness or a lack of 'moral fibre'. Today's society demands a constant readiness to work and socialise, and as a result we often do not want to admit to sleepiness.

Does lack of sleep lead to overload? Without a shadow of a doubt. I have had many stressful periods in my life but I have never felt so overwhelmed, so helpless, so desperate, as when I was trying to cope without proper sleep.

Interestingly, it has been shown that production of the key stress hormone cortisol almost stops when you are asleep. So, not only is your body repairing itself, not only is your mind relaxing and your cells regenerating, but also when you sleep you are having time off from stress. The less time you sleep, the longer you spend awake, and stressed.

Chapter 4

What doesn't work ... and what does

Many of us know we're stressed, we *know* we're overloaded and we are spending a small fortune trying to get out of the trap. The stress-management industry is flourishing. Walk into any spa, any beauty shop or health shop and you will be offered a huge menu of 'stress-busting' treatments and supplements. I'm not saying for a moment that massage or herbs and vitamins can't help stress – and in the next section of the book I'll be suggesting you use some of these techniques as part of the overload solution, but let's be quite clear: they can't remotely *cure* it. We're talking sticking plasters here, short-term solutions. Unless you go further and take a long hard look at your entire life, you will never beat overload, you will merely mask the symptoms a little. The good news is that you don't need to spend more money – the true overload solution won't cost you a penny.

Instant results

We want instant results, we want immediate gratification. If our stress relief comes packaged with nice oils and fluffy towels, we'll go for it. If it requires any kind of effort or any form of deprivation, we'd rather stick with the stress. We're seeing the rise of the ten-minute facial, the five-minute massage. Office managers are cleverly tying people to their desks under the guise of easing stress with 'on-site' massage. Those that do get to the spa are often still so tied into their working life that they won't ever see the real benefit. A PR for a London spa tells me of clients who come in for anti-stress treatments, still talking on the phone. One even dropped her mobile in the floatation tank!

We are willing to try any number of stress-reduction techniques providing they don't involve a serious change to our lifestyle – or even the possibility of *thinking* about change. Many of us are scared to look at what actually causes our stress, our overload. So we will happily buy any number of self-help books and relaxation tapes, stock up on nice smelly candles or 'stress relief' bath oils (few of which even contain active ingredients) but baulk at looking at the real cause of our lifestyle imbalance. In the next section we will be doing just that – but, don't panic, the process is simple and can even be good fun.

Sales of self-help books have rocketed in the last ten years. Yet how many of us really follow them? They've become like diet books, promising the world while the sad truth remains that no book can ever work unless you're willing to change your life, your thoughts, your habitual behaviour, your addictions. Yet we still buy them, because for a moment or two we can kid ourselves that this time it will work. This programme will do the trick. We become addicted to the process of buying, falling in love with each new guru, hoping he or she will sort out our lives. We abnegate responsibility. Then, when it doesn't work, we turn, ever hopeful, to the Next Big Idea. We persuade ourselves that if only we could do time-management, or life coaching we'd sort ourselves out. Yes, managing one's time better is a useful skill – and one we'll look at in the next section – but it isn't the whole of the answer. Some life coaches are excellent, but many will simply add to your overload. Again we're looking for easy answers, for someone to 'sort it out' for us. Above all we yearn for one quick fix. Psychotherapist Sarah Dening says, 'People come to me and say, "I've got a problem. You're the expert. Sort it out." But that's not how it works. How are you ever going to make sense of your life if you're always going to look out there, for someone else to give you the answer?'

It's not stress, as such, we have to cope with, but rather how we relate to stress. Often we are stressed from the inside out, not the outside in. The good news is that you can stop racing around trying to figure out the perfect, number-one treatment, or guru, or cure. Save your money – it won't beat overload. I'll show you simple effective strategies that make *you* your own 'guru'.

Self-help overload?

A deeper question is whether the self-help movement and New Age philosophies are actually *increasing* overload. For the last 20 years we've been drip-fed the belief that we create our own reality, that we are responsible for our own success or failure. Gurus like Anthony Robbins told us we needed to awaken the 'giant within' – so that, just like him, we, too, could transform our lives so we were stinking rich, with a gorgeous body and a stunning partner. Sondra Ray promised we could choose to manifest whatever we wanted in our lives – we could even live forever if we truly wanted. Authors stumbled over one another to tell us we could do it all, have it all, choose the life we want, be whoever we want to be. There were no limits, except the limits of our own imagination and the power of our self-belief.

On the face of it this is good. It empowers us. It tells us that we don't have to lie down and accept our fate, as our ancestors did. We are not stuck in a feudal society in which we are forced to stay knee-deep in the mud, tugging our forelocks as the gentry ride by. We can be whatever and whoever we want. I still believe there is much to be said for a positive outlook, and I'll be showing you ways to self-talk yourself into an empowered state of mind rather than lying down in the middle of the road with 'victim' daubed over your forehead. However, I'll be advising you to choose your positive messages wisely. All too often we're told to affirm the likes of: 'I now choose to be thin'; 'It's safe, fun and exciting to be rich'; 'I deserve a famous rich partner'. We are told to write affirmations for money, to win the lottery, to gain 20 million, to lose 20 pounds. We have been advised to cosmic order for wealth, for a bigger house, a sexier car, a more powerful promotion; to cast prosperity spells, drink love potions and try self-hypnosis for bigger breasts. Creating our own reality has focused purely on the material, on a richer, faster lifestyle. Unfortunately that simply reinforces the message that you need more external possessions, better external circumstances, in order to be happy. As I'll show you, it actually promotes overload.

All the research shows that gaining more money emphatically *does not* increase happiness one jot. Once you get to a certain (pretty low) level of comfortable income, extra money does not turn into extra contentment. Once again, we are tackling stress from the outside in, not the inside out. I'll show you how to shift your thinking, to get beyond the superficial desires, to find out what you *really* need to live a life without overload.

The other problem is, what happens when you bombard your subconscious with your heartfelt desires but your subconscious decides to turn a deaf ear and nothing happens? According to the gurus, you have failed because you have done something wrong; you haven't believed enough, you haven't done enough. Bottom line: you weren't good enough. So you beat yourself up a little bit more. Not a good idea. Self-esteem is one of the keys to beating overload, so in this book I will be advising ways of boosting your self-esteem, not scuppering it.

Bogus spirituality

There is a huge spiritual con going on in modern life. Spirituality has become devalued, as more people jump on the bandwagon realising there are big bucks to be made from cod spirituality. Ancient paths, such as yoga (originally a lifelong search for self-mastery and union with God) have been debased and turned into a trendy pastime. Glossy magazines fall over one another to discover the 'latest yoga' or to shout that gyrotonics, or whatever, is the 'new' yoga. It's no longer enough to wear comfortable clothes and take off your shoes, now you need the smartest yoga gear, the coolest yoga mat in this season's hot colour. In fact you can now buy a Gucci yoga mat for a very unspiritual $850 with its leather carrying case for $350. Laura McCreddie of *Yoga* magazine says, 'It's a statement of who you are. Before it was about your stock portfolio or your aerobics class. Now it's about what yoga mat you carry and whether you practise yoga in a class next to Sadie Frost.'

Whereas true yoga in all its beautiful simplicity yet depth is one of the best stress-busters going, it is no longer a tranquil pursuit if you're spending half your time worrying if you're in the best class or if you're working on the optimum mat. Whatever happened to life-long practice? Choice rears its ugly head again, followed by perfection. Yoga ceases to be a stress-busting activity and, rather, adds to your overload. I'll be talking about yoga and its benefits – and I promise you won't be shelling out a small fortune for a mat.

We now have designer Buddhists, celebrity Christians ... We flirt with different religions, changing allegiance as the fickle tides of celebrity ebb and flow. Or we adopt a pick-'n'-mix attitude to faith – labelling ourselves 'sort of New Age Christian Buddhist' or 'pagan Catholics'. As if we could take the best bits and leave anything we find unpalatable. It's a shame because studies show quite clearly that faith, belonging to a religious group, is a clear protection against the worst excesses of overload. But the studies are talking about bona fide religion, not some cod piecemeal confection.

As Arthur Jeon, in his thought-provoking book *City Dharma*, says, 'Even many of our religions are consumerist in nature, staking out their territory and competing for a share of followers, telling other religions that there is only "one truth".'

Kabbalah is a sad example. I first came across the teachings of the Kabbalah when I was in my early twenties and have studied it ever since. There are huge amounts of quiet wisdom in its teachings, a lifetime's worth of meditation and profound mystical experience. The Kabbalah, although Jewish in origin, is effectively non-denominational – its teachings are outside individual religions (surely a powerful plus in a world riven by religious wars?). Yet, thanks to the infamous Kabbalah Centre, the whole teaching has been tarred with a cynical materialistic brush. Paying a fortune for 'holy' water, for a piece of red string, for books in a language you can't understand, is not Kabbalah, it's a con. It's sympathetic witchcraft – yet no self-respecting witch would dream of charging the kind of sums people are expected to stump up at the Kabbalah Centre.

Any religious institution, any guru, any organisation that wants your money (other than voluntary contributions to charity or for reasonable overheads) is not worth your time, money or soul. Run a mile. In Part Three I'll show you how a genuine, authentic spirituality can shield you from overload – no red string required.

Work as personal growth

Of course, not all of us are seeking meaning and growth in cults and cod religions, or indeed in recognised religion either. The vast majority no longer even consider going to church, temple, mosque or synagogue. Yet the human soul seeks meaning, it cries out for an inner journey, for a move towards self-fulfilment, individuation. If we cannot pursue this quest in a religious sphere, our psyche desperately tries to find somewhere else in which to seek enlightenment. Most of us, nowadays, try to find it at work.

At work, freed from the grind of childcare, cleaning, the need to listen to and support out partners, our spirits and our creativity is free to soar. Surely this is an answer to overload? If we can find happiness and meaning at work, surely we have found the Holy Grail? As we will see in Part Three, discovering what makes your 'soul sing' at work is a vital part of overcoming overload. However, you have to be careful that work does not become the be all and end all of life. Even the perfect job can still lead to burnout, to meltdown, to vicious overload.

Companies big and small are also plugging into the self-help movement, realising that they can keep their workers happy and committed by turning workplace into workshop, by helping people 'find themselves' through their work. I do believe that some companies truly are trying their best to keep their employees happy. But many others are jumping onto the self-development bandwagon, realising that this is a smart new way to keep their workforce productive and obedient.

We're seeing the rise of the 'addicted employee', who is so obsessed with his or her work and workplace that there is no life outside of work. Madeleine Bunting investigates, in *Willing Slaves*, the incredible work culture of companies like Microsoft and Orange, where employees are pushed to the limit – and beyond. Her concern is that such companies are demanding more than it is reasonable to expect from anyone, that the very concept of any kind of work-life balance has been tossed out of the window – the job is all. There are no boundaries, no limits to the expectations. Human beings are overloaded when they have to stay 'on-message' all the time, when their souls are sucked into living out a mission statement 24/7, when they become a part of the corporate brand. There is no freedom here – just more servitude.

Drugs and drink ... and more work

It's pretty obvious that the classic avoidance techniques don't work either. Nearly one in four adults in the UK drink to 'self-medicate' themselves against stress and depression. Dr Massimo Riccio of the Priory Group commissioned a study that said that 'Alcohol abuse has become an acceptable part of British life' and that the proportion of people dependent on alcohol is worryingly high. Many people also use marijuana to 'de-stress' after a tough day while others use designer drugs to boost mood and energy after an exhausting day.

Many thousands of people take 'happy pills' such as the anti-depressant SSRIs (selective serotonin reuptake inhibitors) to combat depression and low mood, often brought on by overload. I happen to think that properly prescribed anti-depressants can be a valuable short-term solution for *severely* depressed people. However, they can mask the underlying problem and allow people to continue overloaded lives beyond the point where their minds and bodies would usually tell them to stop. They dampen the symptoms but rarely solve the problem. In fact, study after study has shown that short-term counselling or psychotherapy is as effective as medication for easing mild or moderate depression. Yet once again we look for the easy option. Simpler to pop a pill than confront the real reasons for your depression.

....

Holidays – an escape from overload?

Many of us run away to escape, going on vacation and taking short breaks to escape the stress. I personally know over-loaded professionals who take six or seven holidays a year –

and yet remain stressed and unhappy. Escaping isn't the answer. Indeed researchers at Israel's Tel Aviv University found that any sense of relaxation and happiness you might get from a holiday faded just three days after returning to work. Levels of stress and burnout returned within a mere three weeks. And that was for those who resisted the temptation to keep 'in touch' via pagers, mobiles, laptops, radio and TV. If you can't even switch off on holiday, the results will be even more dismal.

Running away is not the answer. Distracting yourself with the latest cult therapy or religion won't work either. In the next section of this book we'll look at what really *does* work. I'll show you simple yet effective techniques for time- and money-management. I'll show you how to beat the various demons of overload and take back control. I'll give you ten strategies that are *guaranteed* to lessen overload, overnight. Excited? You should be. This is your chance to take back control over your life. Let's get started.

Part Two

*Short-term Fixes –
Band-Aid for the Stressed
Soul*

Chapter 5
The fork in the crossroads

Now we're going to get stuck in and work out some practical ways of coping with overload, of taking back some of the control that overload inevitably erodes. It's not easy. Many of us are quietly addicted to our overloaded lives. Others have become so mired in the myth of overload that we have simply surrendered to it. We throw up our hands and say we have no choice, that we have to react to the world the way it is – and the world is based on overload.

Well, yes and no. It's certainly true that our society is in love with speed, overwork and status. We are also a paranoid society. Our world consists of employers who think (erroneously, as it happens) that allowing people to work within sensible limits will lose their business advantage. It also consists of workers who keep an eye on their colleagues to see who is working longer rather than smarter. However (and it's a big however), it does not have to be this way. We do have choices. Admittedly some of us have less leeway in our choices than others; for example, if you're a single working parent without a support system, overload is probably indelibly written into your life description. Nevertheless, most of us can arrange our lives to lessen overload (and there is even hope for the single working parents amongst you).

What would you do to help yourself?

I'd like you to be totally and brutally honest now, as you think about this question:

How much of your overload is created by yourself?

Many of us allow overload to happen. It's not always conscious but, if we can be honest, it is down to us. But if we want to beat overload, we have some tough choices to make. For example:

- Would you be willing to have less money in order to lessen overload?
- Would you be willing to trade your prestigious job for peace of mind?
- Would you downshift your house, your car, your lifestyle for more time with your family?
- Would you be willing to lose status to find balance?
- Would you be willing to upset a few people by saying no to their demands?

Think about it? *Would* you? If you are honest enough to say, 'No, I wouldn't' then I guarantee you won't be alone. As economist Gregg Easterbrook says pragmatically in *The Progress Paradox*, 'People are willing to bear stress in return for acquisitions.' I'm not saying that wanting things, per se, is wrong. But it is important to be clear about what you are doing, and why you are doing it. If you overwork, for example, are you really doing it 'for the family' or because, in your heart of hearts, you get a kick out of working, or you prefer to avoid the heavy home stuff? If you downshifted your job, would you miss the warm glow your high status bestows on you? What would you actually do with the extra time you would save if you weren't addicted to email, texting, your mobile, television, the Internet?

The exercises that follow are intended to help you find some clarity about your own overload situation. When you are overloaded it can be hard to find time. I know it's tough, but take an evening out: turn off the television, the computer, the mobile and turn on the voicemail. Have a shower or bath and spend a few minutes just breathing calmly and deeply (so that you switch off from everyday panic and subconsciously take yourself into a calmer, more focused state of mind). Then do the following exercises carefully, giving them real thought. Don't censor yourself; put down everything that comes into your mind.

Your life as a circle

This is a useful exercise at this point because it allows you to see, very graphically, how overload is affecting the balance of your life.

1. Take a large sheet of paper and write down all the roles you play (or would like to play) in your life. So, for instance, I would write: worker, mother, wife, daughter, sister, aunt, friend, book reader, exerciser, artist, spiritual person, gardener, would-be novelist. Plus, if I were honest: TV watcher and social emailer.

2. Now draw a large circle on another piece of paper and divide it into segments, according to how much time each 'role' takes in your life. When I first did this I was shocked at how far work ruled my life (see the chart overleaf). I could also see, quite clearly, that while I moaned about not having time to see my friends, or do my art, I could merrily spend a sizeable proportion of my time watching television or punching out emails.

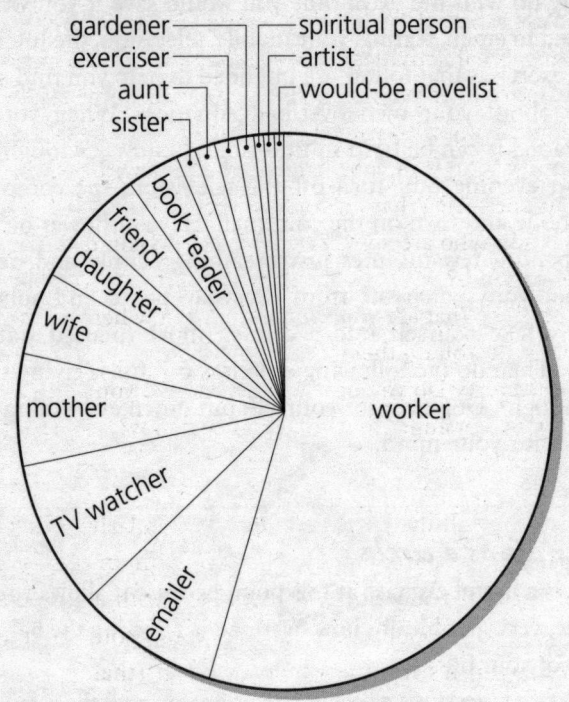

3. Once you have seen your life imbalance, draw another circle and map out how your life might look if it were in balance. Try it. It can be a real eye-opener.

Looking at your life

Next, make an inventory of your life. Take six sheets of paper and write a heading on top of each. Then underneath, in a list, answer the following questions in as much detail as possible.

1. **Work** What do you do (be precise and list every part of your work)? Whom do you see (on a daily and more occasional basis)? Where do you go for work (do you stay in one place or move around)?

2. **Home** Where do you live? What do you do in your home (what activities)? How much time do you spend in your home? Whom do you see in your home (either people living with you or visitors)?

3. **Family** Who is in your family (who lives with you and who doesn't)? What do you do together?

4. **Friends** Who are your friends? What do you do with your friends?

5. **Hobbies** What are your hobbies? When, where and with whom do you do them?

6. **Spirituality** Do you have any beliefs? Do you go to a place of worship? Do you meditate or pray?

Now underline all the parts that work particularly well with a green pen, all the parts that are bearable with an orange pen, and the bits that really don't work for you with a red pen. Be brutally honest – nobody needs to see this but you. You may be surprised, often it's not the whole situation (that is, work or family) that is the problem but merely elements of it.

Some solutions might be immediately obvious. Others may well become clearer given time. Keep it light; play with ways of reducing overload. What might you do?

Three steps to reduce overload

Now, you have to be like a gardener: taking a sharp pair of secateurs and cutting back the overgrowth. You can either be brutal, slicing off huge chunks, or you can take a softly-softly approach, trimming a little bit off here and there. It doesn't really matter – all that is important is that you find some way of easing the load on your time.

Overload, in the very simplest terms, means you have: (a) Too much to do; and (b) Too little time in which to do it.

Let's start with too much to do. There are three basic ways of cutting down your load:

1. Delegate
2. Share
3. Shed

The first two call for a support system. In the past we would have been supported and helped by a close-knit family and community. Nowadays most of us have to find alternative support systems, usually comprising friends, colleagues, even strangers. At this stage, it doesn't really matter from where your support comes, only that it does come. Many of us seem to think it's somehow brave to struggle solo, so we haul huge weights on to our shoulders, like modern-day Atlases. Where is it written that it's weak or selfish to have help? Of course, many of us have been taught from an early age that it's rude to say no; that it's good to be stoical, to cope regardless of how much is piled onto us. If you know that this is a particular problem for you, we'll look at ways of getting over it later in the book. For now, I'd like you to concentrate on these three practical ways of cutting your load.

1. Delegate

Some of us are lucky enough to have a dream team behind us. Some people have personal assistants, secretaries, housekeepers, cleaners, gardeners, nannies, and so on. Ironically, the people who do have help often don't take full advantage of it. I can't count the number of times I've seen people clean before their cleaner comes, or hover over the gardener, directing the pulling up of every weed. Let go.

At work another dynamic comes into play. Many people don't dare to relinquish control over any aspect of their work. Consequently they are scared of delegation and keep their workload unnecessarily high. Be honest: are you scared of delegating? If so, what is your fear? Is it reasonable or imaginary? If you have this god-given opportunity for shedding some of your workload legitimately, take it with both hands.

The majority of us, of course, don't have a dream team or even one loyal cohort. However, there are still opportunities for delegation. Many people (women in particular) put in a full day's work and then come home to look after children, cook meals, clean, and so on.

> *Nicky*, a journalist and mother, was putting in long stressful days at the office and then coming home to start another 'job', cleaning the house, cooking the food, dealing with homework and bedtime. I persuaded her to sit down with her husband and look at how their home chores were shared out. Were they fairly shared? No. Time to delegate. Fortunately, Tim, her husband, was willing to play ball. He agreed to take on the cooking, and clean the bathrooms and floors. They take it in turns to supervise homework and put the children to bed while the other goes to the gym or catches up on work.

If you read that and think: dream on – my partner would never do that, I'd suggest you both need to look at your relationship. I'll give advice on communication later in the book.

Interestingly, a lot of people insist on taking on all the work. They will make excuses such as, 'If I left it to my husband, it wouldn't get done' or, 'If the children did it, I'd just have to do it again.' If this is you, think about your reasons. Are you a perfectionist? Maybe time to let go a little. Are you playing the martyr? Are you being a control freak? Ask yourself why. Deep questions. If your finances permit it, call in help. Cleaning, laundry and ironing services are godsends, providing they are reliable and hassle-free. Doing your own tax is a pain – hand it over to an accountant. Teenagers are always desperate for cash and can be co-opted for mundane tasks.

2. Share

Some parts of life can't be delegated, but they can be shared. This particularly comes into play when you have children. Juggling childcare and work is probably the major nightmare for most working parents. Even if you don't work (and have small children or babies) you will find it impossible to have any kind of 'time-out'. If you can't afford childcare, you have to be creative. One of the most effective ways is to build up a small group of fellow parents in similar situations. I say small, because nobody needs the stress of a huge gang of (mainly somebody else's) children. This set-up can work in a variety of ways: car-pooling for the school run; an informal 'after-school club' at varying houses; babysitting pool, and so on. You will need to be organised and pick your fellow parents with care – if you don't share the same values, thoughts on diet, behaviour and manners, and so on, you're in trouble. Many parents naturally meet up with like-minded, similarly stressed people at play-group, the school gate or so on. If not, you will have to be more proactive – ask your head teacher to put you in touch with suitable parents or talk to your health visitor (via your doctor's surgery).

Fiona, a working mother with two young children, couldn't afford a nanny and had a daily scrabble to get after-school care. Then she clubbed together with two other families for a part-time 'nanny-share'. Each week operations move to a different house, with the resident parents responsible for providing supplies. Costs are minimised and the children love the 'club' set-up.

Other parts of life are open to sharing, too. Cleaning is a bore, so make it a family affair. Do a heavy-duty clean once a week *en famille.*

Alice and David both work full-time and have three children. They make do during the week with cursory tidying up, and every Sunday have a full-on family assault on the house. Everyone picks chores; they put on energy-inspiring music and work like demons for a few hours before having a slap-up brunch as a reward for the hard work.

Alternatively, housework can be done throughout the week, with everyone taking charge of specific duties. It might be tough to begin with (if you have let your family get away with it for years) but it's not impossible. Explain the situation, get everyone to choose their chores from a list, and resist the urge to redo imperfect dusting.

It's also worth taking a look at your work. Are there any tasks there that could reasonably be shared? It's not written in stone that a task must be done by one person and one person alone. Whereas dumping the dreaded work on another person (delegating) might be unfair or resisted, it could be quite reasonable to get together a group of people to share the work. This works particularly well on small, silly tasks that nonetheless eat into your time – such as making coffee, photocopying minutes, covering reception, and so on. In one early admin job I had, I successfully 'shared' out so much of my work, I found myself with barely anything left to do.

3. Shed

This is the tough one. Take a deep breath and let your mind roam around the possibility of letting certain things go. Look back at your list – are there any parts of your life that aren't strictly essential *and* which don't give you particular pleasure? For example, there's no point in cutting out your yoga class (providing you enjoy it) or the one night a week when you see your best mate. However, think about these questions:

- Are there parts of your work that aren't strictly necessary or useful?
- Are there things you do out of (possibly misplaced) duty?

We are creatures of habit and often continue with patterns of behaviour long after they have served their purpose. We also often keep up with various duties or acquaintances because we feel we ought to. The easiest way to figure these out is to watch your language – whenever you say, 'I must …' 'I ought …' or 'I have to …' you're talking about duty. Obviously some duties are necessary obligations but, if you're honest, you'll find that there are things you don't really *have* to do but feel you should. It sounds brutal but sometimes the best thing you can do is simply to drop a few commitments.

- What drags you down or takes time that you'd rather use in other ways?
- Which activities make your heart sink?

It might be a question of degree.

Much of our overload comes about because we feel resentment about unfair commitments. Figure out how much is fair – and stick to it (we'll look at how to say no later on in the book).

> **Beth**, a successful solicitor and mother, found she was going out virtually every night of the week, networking with colleagues, ostensibly to find new business and 'get her face around'. She never saw her daughter or partner and felt drained and resentful. Then she reframed the situation. She decided that she would go out twice a week maximum and say a firm 'No' when cajoled into doing more. 'At first it was quite scary,' she admits. 'I was worried I would be perceived as not being able to take the pace.' But her colleagues soon accepted the new status quo and she is just as effective at work and much more relaxed at home.

Reframe stress

Stress expert Vera Peiffer says, 'Life is ten per cent what happens to you and 90 per cent how you react to it.' She's spot-on. After you have taken steps to reduce your physical overload as far as possible, the rest comes down mainly to attitude. You can decide whether to be stressed or whether to stay calm.

Start by questioning your beliefs about your overload and stress.

- What are the negative or limiting beliefs that are holding you back?
- What are you scared of?

We'll work with this throughout the book but for now just allow yourself the possibility of change. Play with the idea of

not being a stressed overloaded person.
- *If* I were calm, I would be able to …
- *If* I were brave, I would …

What would you do? How might you do it? What would it be like to be a calm, centred person, in full control of your life? How would you be?

Make a change today

Is there one tiny change you could dare to make today? Try it. Start small, shore up your successes and move on to the medium challenges. Are you already baulking, thinking it will be hard? Challenge that assumption, too. Why should life always be hard? What would it be like if it were easy? It's a curious thing, but people who expect the world to work for them, find it does. Those who expect the worst, usually get it. It's to do with the fact that our subconscious tries to mirror our thoughts and expectations – it literally attracts our beliefs to us. Incredible thought, isn't it?

Yes, you can change the way you think. Learned optimism can work wonders on your life. If you feel you can't do something, pretend you can – fake it. Tell yourself, 'If I could do this, I would …'

Try not to put your negative expectations on the day. So many of us wake up thinking, 'this is going to be an awful day'. What if it weren't? Tell yourself you will cope with each part of the day as and when it happens. What's the point in wasting time and energy on something that hasn't happened yet? Tell yourself, 'Right now, I'm fine.' Repeat it like a mantra throughout your day, and it works a charm. I use it when I have to undergo some ordeal such as driving in thick snow or ice; instead of panicking about what *might* happen, I tell myself that 'right now' I am doing great, I'm fine. I'll return to this later on in the book.

If you know you are prone to deep negative thinking, play the 'worst-case scenario' game. If the very worst happened, what would you do? How would you cope? Be specific and practical. Most worst-case scenarios have practical solutions or coping strategies. Now it's time to look at the second part of the overload problem: too little time.

Chapter 6

Winning back time

We've looked at the 'too much to do' question so now we need to look at 'too little time'. Time is our greatest modern enemy. We try to 'make time' and 'save time' but, on the whole, we mainly 'don't have time' or 'run out of time'. We live our lives by the clock, counting seconds, panicking about how little time we have, worrying about how we can cram more and more into the same number of hours. We blame ourselves for our failure to cope. We think that if only we were better at managing our time, we wouldn't be so overloaded. To be honest, I think the real problem lies deeper than that. All the time-management courses in the world won't be able to balance too many commitments – it just doesn't add up. However, time-management does offer some very useful tips and techniques for making yourself more efficient, for making your time more productive. There are also other practical ways of clawing back time. You may read them and think: 'but I don't have time to do that'. Please try. I promise that by clearing clutter, getting organised and setting goals you will save yourself *huge* amounts of time in the long run. Even more, your mind will feel in control and you will be far less stressed.

Clear the clutter

If your home and workplace are neck-high in mess, there is no way you can keep yourself calm and focused. It is impossible to relax in messy spaces – so you will be adding an additional layer of stress. On a psychological level clutter irritates the mind; it reminds us of things which need doing, fixing, finishing, starting even. We are problem-solving creatures, and if our mind catches sight of unfinished projects or huge 'to-do' piles or even bulging closets, it will become bothered and stressed. When the world around you skids 'out of control' your mind will shortly follow. Personally, I don't think anyone can start to sort out his or her life while they are in a mess, which is why I always suggest people start to get their heads straight by putting their external environment in order first.

Clearing your home and office will make a huge difference to your time. Put aside a weekend to tackle the mess. Go through each and every room and be brutal. Remember, too, it's not a case of 'out of sight, out of mind'; you need to go beyond cosmetic anti-clutter and check all those hidden places, too: behind the sofa; in your closets and cupboards; drawers and dressers; attics, cellars and sheds. It may not be noticeable on a physical level but psychologically it's still clutter and you know it's there, however subconsciously, and it's affecting you.

I won't go into the precise details of clutter clearing. There have been plenty of books and TV shows taking you through the process. If you do want more information check out my earlier book *Spirit of the Home*, which describes the process in detail.

Get organised

The next step is to sort what's left into some kind of meaningful order. Confusion contributes significantly to overload.

Every house needs its own 'essential papers' file, containing insurance policies, mortgage documents, investments, tax details, licences and guarantees, and so on, all neatly filed away. Use box files or a filing cabinet for other essential reference material (but make sure it really is essential). Go through your files once a year and check they are still valid.

Offices need to be tidy and uncluttered, too. Once you have cleared your office and desk, you should need to spend only about ten minutes a week keeping the next load of clutter at bay.

Keep a diary and a calendar

The calendar needs to be one of those large ones with plenty of space for each day. Put it in a central place and make sure your partner enters his or her appointments and engagements (so you don't clash). Don't have more than one calendar or you will get into a mess. Transfer information from the central home calendar into your personal diary so you know what's going on. If you have a secretary at work, or someone else manages your time, then start every day by letting him or her transfer important home dates into your work diary. Make them sacrosanct.

Identify your goals

Goal-setting can be about hitting deadlines, about seeing more of your family, about moving towards working in a different place or in a different way, about finding time for regular exercise. It can also be about reducing or banishing overload.

The key is to spend a regular set time checking goals – a few minutes each day and every week, a little longer each month, and maybe set aside a day a year for long-term goals. Make them clearly defined, realistic but challenging, and set a manageable timescale for achieving them. Break down large tasks into manageable chunks and set subdeadlines. We often become overwhelmed and overloaded because we expect instant or near-instant results. If you want to lose weight sensibly, for example, you would aim to lose between a half and one kilo (one or two pounds) a week. If a child has a list of 20 words to learn for school next week, run through three each day rather than trying to gobble them all down on Sunday night. Goals and sensible chunking down save you from last-minute panics and enable you to manage your workload without stress.

You can refine this further for really huge or overwhelming tasks. Time-management calls this process 'eating elephants':

Question: how do you eat an elephant?

Answer: a little bit at a time.

So, first divide your 'elephant' into 'bitesize' pieces and include regular bites in your schedule. Secondly, make sure you 'eat' a bite every day, in addition to your other tasks. Finally, make sure you finish your elephant and don't take on more than one or two elephants at a time. For example, if you wanted to learn Japanese, you would not only schedule-in your weekly classes but also commit yourself to learning ten new words a day. It doesn't sound much but by the end of the year you would have learnt 3,650 new words.

Planning

Once you know what you want to do, you can concentrate on how to do it.

As with your goals you should aim to set aside periods for planning. Again, do this regularly – every year (for an overview), monthly (for middle-distance), weekly (for closer focus) and daily (for an action plan). Ask yourself what you want to get out of the period ahead, what are your goals, your most important tasks, how much time you have already committed (such as, to holidays, courses, family, meetings) and what long-term large projects you have. It's important to get your priorities straight when you are planning. What is really important in your life? What must come before anything else? All too often we fall into overload because work pushes its nose in first. Over-committed on the work front, we are left trying to squeeze everything else into the scraps of time left over.

Block out time for holiday and birthdays. Throw in a few family or 'off with friends' weekends. Slot in some 'me' time. You may not use all of it, but if you don't put it in, you definitely won't have any of it.

Include the family

If you have a family, it's a really good habit to have everyone join in with these sessions. It brings families together and avoids that awful 'I didn't know you wanted to do this or that' syndrome. It also helps to keep partners on track.

When we're overloaded we rarely take the time to talk slowly, carefully or considerately to our partners about what we want in our lives, about what works and what doesn't. If you can identify (both individual and shared) goals together and plan together, it makes your needs far more concrete and opens up the possibility of compromise and sharing.

A planning session a day

This is so very simple yet it will *instantly* improve your life. Having a clear plan for the day ahead focuses the mind and puts you in control like nothing else. Incidentally, this isn't just for work, homemakers will find it just as useful. You will need either one of those diaries that details the hours of the day – or you can simply use a large sheet of paper with the hours marked down the left-hand side.

- First throw out all those endless 'to do' lists – they overload the mind and make you panic.
- Just before you finish work (or at the end of your day) ask yourself what regular scheduled tasks or meetings you have for tomorrow. Block them off in your diary.
- What is your major task, what *must* you do tomorrow? Set aside a realistic block of time (err on the side of caution). Be precise – for instance, block out the slots between 9 and 11 am and then 3 to 4.30 pm.
- Put in specific times for making phone calls and reading/answering emails. It is far more time-effective to do these in blocks rather than breaking concentration and doing them ad hoc. Check emails twice or three times a day maximum.
- If you have time left, you can schedule in other tasks, but be realistic about what time they would take.
- Make a short list of brief one-off tasks (non-urgent phone calls/letters/emails/birthday cards) that could be slotted in. If you find you have over-estimated your time and have a few spare minutes, use them for these tasks.
- Remember to add in travelling time, lunch and relaxation breaks (yes, these are *vitally* important, even if they are only five-minute breaks).

At the end of the day, spend a few minutes getting everything ready for the next day: set out clothes, get children to pack lunch-boxes, put out sports gear, pack work bag with papers, keys, travel card, and so on.

Effective time-management is about giving yourself and the people you work and live with better quality time; it is not about running your life like a boot camp. Used properly it should mean that you find you have more time at your fingertips and enable you to work effectively, to get out with friends and play with your children, to work steadily towards fulfilling your goals and still have time to collapse on the sofa on a Sunday afternoon without feeling guilty.

Time stealers versus time savers

Try to follow these principles – they will make a huge difference.

The time stealers

- **The phone** Keep calls during work hours short and to the point. Set aside phone-free periods for tasks that need concentration, and bunch all your calls into set phone periods (this includes mobiles, too). Use voicemail to screen calls, and phone back in your own time.
- **Email** Don't stay permanently on-line (the bleep of incoming mail is too much for most of us to resist). Check and respond to emails at set times of the day.
- **The Internet** Keep searches focused and have a time limit. Resist the temptation to surf aimlessly or get hauled into chat rooms and bulletin boards – *major* time stealers.
- **Drop-in visitors** Make it clear when you welcome visitors and when not. Be polite but firm: say something like, 'This isn't a good time for me. Could we get together at four o'clock instead?'
- **Inefficient meetings** What is the meeting for? How long does it need to take? Is it really necessary? Do you really need to be there? Be clear, concise and set a time limit.
- **Disorganisation** Lack of planning, lack of priorities, papers all over the desk. Keep clear, focused, direct and tidy.
- **Inability to say 'no'** Are you scared of offending people? Do you take on far more than you can logistically cope with? If

you know how much available time you have you can judge whether you can take on more work. If not, then say so clearly and politely.

- **Lack of self-discipline** You know you should be doing that report but you'll just have a small break, just make a quick call, just have lunch ... Give yourself deadlines and stick to them, using your daily plan.

The time savers

- **A clear desk** Keep on your desk only the thing you are actually working on. Do the same for your home – clear, uncluttered, everything in the right place.
- **A large rubbish bin** Look at each piece of paper as it arrives and make a decision about it. Either deal with it, file it or bin it – immediately.
- **Schedule 'me' time** Allow yourself certain periods each day when you won't be disturbed. Use them for dealing with elephant tasks, for creative work or ideas, or simply for sitting quietly and refuelling.
- **Become proactive rather than reactive** Decide what you will do and when. Plan what you will do and when; treat 'appointments' with yourself just as you would appointments with someone else, breaking them only if absolutely unavoidable.
- **Take stretch breaks every hour** Walk around for a few minutes or do some yoga, and you will return refreshed and with your concentration replenished.
- **Are you an early bird or night owl?** When are you most creative, most organised? Schedule your day accordingly. Use your 'off' times to do emails and catch up on small tasks.

Be low-maintenance and proud!

It seems to be a badge of pride in our warped consumer society that we be 'high-maintenance'. That's all well and good if you're a time-happy celebrity who can fritter away half the day in the gym or the spa. However, if you're a normal woman (this one is mainly for women) who is running short on time, high-maintenance becomes yet another stress factor in your life. Try going low-maintenance for a change:

- Get an easy, get-up-and-go hairstyle. Imagine a life without endless blow-drying, flattening or styling. Go for a short, sexy crop or keep long hair tied back in a super-cool, slicked-back ponytail. Buy a fabulous wig for those tumbling-lock moments.
- Opt for a work 'uniform' to ease the habitual 'what the hell shall I wear?' dilemma. Many of the world's high flyers and Uber-businesswomen have a series of classic black suits for work. Jazz them up with coloured tops and fabulous accessories.
- Ditch dark nail varnishes and opt for pale or clear nail colour – or leave your nails nude. You could spend hours a week keeping bright-red polish looking good.
- Have your eyelashes and eyebrows professionally tinted and your eyebrows shaped. Then, if you don't have time for full make-up, you can dash on some lipstick and you're done.
- Keep your beauty rituals simple. You really don't need all those scrubs, packs, polishes and four different creams for each section of your face. Honestly. In fact, you could be doing your skin a disservice, as you'll be piling on the chemicals and causing it stress. Pick a beauty brand that doesn't stuff its products full of chemicals (I like Dr Hauschka, Jurlique, REN, Spiezia and Weleda). Then simply cleanse (a cream cleanser will take off make-up, too); wash your face thoroughly; use a toner if you wish; and

moisturise. That's it. Once in a while treat yourself to a professional facial for all the extra stuff.

- Use one handbag. There is nothing more irritating that finding you have left half the important stuff in the other bag.

More esoteric thoughts on time

We may be ruled by time, but it's worth remembering that time is a man-made device. We set up the clocks. We set the deadly deadlines.

Psychotherapist and author Will Parfitt suggests some intriguing exercises for looking at your relationship with time. I found them enlightening and so offer them here for you to try.

Doing time: a sentence for life

Will suggests you ask yourself this question: are you doing your time or is your time doing you? Consider: who is doing your time?

Doing time, of course, is the vernacular for being in prison where a life sentence is, clearly, the longest sentence possible. A sentence is also what a judge bestows on the convicted. Of course, a sentence is additionally a group of words that expresses a thought, feeling or idea. With this in mind, ask yourself: what's *your* life sentence?

It might be something like: there's never enough time; time flies and waits for no one; I wish there were more hours in the day; I can never keep up; time's a bitch; and so on. Write out your life sentence clearly (in just one sentence) before continuing. Now ask yourself how you might reframe your original sentence? For example, there's always more than enough time; time is my trusted companion who never leaves my side; each day is perfect in itself; I go at my own pace; and so on.

What's your new life sentence?

Time to ...

There are just three short commands for this activity. Look at each phrase and consider what interpretation it has in your life. Give yourself a couple of minutes with each before continuing to the next. It *is* a strange, even disconcerting, exercise but just try it.

1. Time line
2. Time out
3. Time up

What did you come up with? Possible interpretations for some people might be:

1. Time line = life
2. Time out = retirement, illness, positive breaks
3. Time up = death

What do you want to do before it's time up? Start thinking.

Winning back time

As you do these exercises, I hope that you will become more aware of your own relationship with time. How far is timing ruling your life? Are you willing to let yourself be at its beck and call? Is it time to change your thoughts about time? You may find it interesting to think back to the lessons you learnt as a child about time. Why are you always late, or hate being late? Why are you always rushed, never having enough time? Are these perceptions and beliefs that you learnt when you were young and never questioned? By becoming proactive, deciding where your priorities lie, and how you will use the time you have, you can gain a much larger degree of control over your life.

Chapter 7

Ten dramatic ways to reduce overload overnight

The title of this chapter is no vain boast. If you put all ten suggestions into practice, you *will* reduce your overload, dramatically and pretty well instantly. You might not be ready to take all ten on board, but if you just try one, it will help. Two would be great. The more you try, the better you will feel.

Let's look at the list:

1. Turn off your mobile

When you're in control of your mobile, it's a useful tool. When it starts to control your life, it becomes destructive. I'm not saying ditch your mobile, all I'm saying is choose when you answer it. So, for the most part, keep it turned off. This will be tough because people will have become accustomed to being able to get hold of you 24/7. If you are constantly on the move and you have children, you will want their school or carers to be able to contact you. Fine – have a dedicated mobile for that purpose and that purpose alone.

Otherwise, check your messages and texts at set points during the day (the times scheduled for making calls) and respond to them during that time. If, at this stage, you can't envisage turning off your mobile for very long periods, ease yourself into it. Turn it off when you meet people (give them your full attention). Practise when you are on journeys (your fellow travellers will be grateful). Switch it off as soon as you get home (your family will be delighted). Pretty soon you will find that people will stop relying on getting hold of you instantly. They might even think twice about trying to contact you 'out of hours'.

Question your addiction to your mobile. Why it is so important to be contactable at any time? What is your fear? How did you cope before you had a mobile? How much of your mobile talk time/text time is really essential and how much is social gossip? If you enjoy the banter of the phone or text, that's fine – but recognise this and watch out that it remains pleasurable and doesn't become stressful. Be wise enough to recognise that some things are better said in person. Let's not go the way of Malaysia that has had to ban divorce via text message, eh?

2. Unplug the TV

TV has become sacred, the god of so many households. When I wrote my book, *Spirit of the Home*, I talked about how, in the past, the hearth was the centre of the home where people would gather to share stories, experiences, day-to-day life. The original hearth was circular (a symbol of unity, completion). Nowadays the heart of most modern homes is the television set, the box. It is square and we sit, not around it, but facing it (usually below it), like passive, obedient schoolchildren listening to teacher. Generally we sit in silence, eyes glued to the screen, oblivious of the people who may be around us.

I am not saying never watch TV. However, if you want to ease overload, you should be very discriminating in your viewing.

Television is addictive. The more you watch, the more you want to watch.

The time you spend watching television could be spent in other, more creative ways – ways that actively reduce overload. If you weren't watching television you could, for example, find time for doing some yoga, or taking up an art class, or playing with your children, or talking with your partner, or just gazing out of the window. Secondly, the content of most television programmes encourages several of the overload 'demons' mentioned in the first part of the book. We're fed a constant diet of shows that dwell on perfection and fuel expectation. No wonder we overload our lives as we desperately scrabble to emulate what we see on television.

Thirdly, many television programmes focus on natural catastrophes, violent crime and gross negativity. I'm not saying you shouldn't be concerned or interested in the world around us, but you do need to keep a perspective, and TV (because it is such an immediate, engrossing medium) does not encourage perspective.

Television taming

How do you nudge your TV viewing into balance? Look through the listings once a week and decide – ahead of time – if there are programmes that are really worth watching. Then, just watch that programme – or tape it to watch at a time of your choice. Or start small by having designated 'no TV' days and arrange to do other things instead. Or, be bold and brave, and follow the advice of astrologer and life coach Michael Geary who says categorically, 'Turn off the damn TV.'

3. Make a media embargo

Most of us devour huge amounts of newsprint every week. Is it necessary? No. Does it overload us? Undoubtedly. It takes time away from other activities and can often make us feel stressed, distressed or inadequate.

We all feel that somehow we *ought to* read the paper every day. Some of us go further and read several, despite the fact that most papers report the same stories (albeit with different biases). Of course we should be informed about our world – but (unless your job specifically entails knowing a bit about everything all the time) the news barrage just isn't necessary. Do you really want to burden yourself with the worries of the world?

Cut down on your news intake. Skim the headlines on the Internet, if you must, on a daily basis. Buy a good quality news round up on a weekly or monthly basis to stay in touch with the important issues. Newspapers go in for scaremongering on a large scale. If you peruse the newspapers regularly you should be aware that you will be inviting panic, worry and anxiety into your life on a daily basis.

When you buy a glossy magazine, bear in mind that it receives most of its revenue from advertising. Effectively you are buying a glossy catalogue – urging you (depending on your age or gender) to buy new clothes, make-up, cars, furnishings, gadgets, toys, food, *stuff*.

You will also be fed a diet of features telling you how to change your life – because (the implication goes) your life is nowhere near good enough as it should (or could) be. Magazines fuel expectation and status envy, and one of the most pernicious ways they do this is in their relentless portrayal of 'ideal' men and women. As a result we become further obsessed with perfection, and in pursuit of that perfection we starve ourselves, drug ourselves, poison ourselves and even lie down and let ourselves be cut open and stitched back together again. How mad is this? To be fair, some magazines are trying – but maybe not hard enough. Yes, there is the odd fashion spread using 'real' (in other words, normal-sized) women instead of stick-thin models. Yes, there is the occasional feature bemoaning the rise of eating disorders. But these are sandwiched between the latest wonder-diet and shock horror exposés of celebrities with cellulite. Again, I'm not saying ditch your favourite mags, but just become aware of the game they play.

4. Go on an Internet diet

As a writer, I adore the Internet – it allows me to work from a house stuck on a hill in the middle of nowhere. It also allows me to keep in touch with friends who are scattered to the four winds. But it is my personal addiction and I have learnt to be careful. If you are anything like me, impose strict limits on your Internet use. The issue here is mainly one of time – I know people who are literally typing their lives away staring at a screen. Of course, other issues may come into play: a lot of information on the web is not accurate and you can easily scaremonger yourself into unnecessary anxiety. Then again, if you find yourself tempted by on-line sex sites and chat rooms you could be playing with fire – and your relationship. If you get hooked on eBay and shopping sites, your finances will almost certainly suffer.

Choose specific times of day for receiving and responding to email (as detailed in the previous chapter). Be strict with yourself. Limit your on-line browsing. Cut down or break free from on-line groups. Being 'always on' can affect your productivity (and create overload) as our brains can really cope with only one thing at a time. Interesting new research from the University of London showed that texting and emailing throughout the working day can 'fog your brain' as much as smoking cannabis, knocking ten points off your IQ. It's been dubbed 'infomania' and comes about when your mind is in an almost permanent state of readiness to react to our 'always-on' technology instead of focusing on the task in hand. Be warned.

5. Cut out caffeine

Caffeine is supremely addictive – if you have ever tried to give it up you will have most likely suffered awful withdrawal headaches. Fortunately it clears from your body within a few days. But our psychological dependence on caffeine (and remember it's not just in coffee but also in tea, chocolate and cola) is subtler. Why give up coffee? Because virtually every overloaded person relies on it – and yet it actually *increases* overload. Yes, a shot of espresso will make you more alert, more awake, more energised – but only for a short time. Then your energy levels will slump down lower than before and you will need another 'fix'. Caffeine also places strain on the adrenal glands, it puts you on unnecessary 'red alert' and so you're caught in that twilight stress response zone. Researchers at Duke University in the USA have found that drinking coffee in the morning can lead to increases in blood pressure, feelings of stress, and elevated stress hormone levels throughout the day and even into the evening. So it's small wonder that caffeine also interferes with your sleep. It's easy to get caught in the vicious circle of poor sleep leading to feeling tired leading to drinking coffee leading to another poor night's sleep and so on.

Just one cup of coffee can elevate cortisol levels above normal, and these can remain high for at least two days. Why should you worry? 'When cortisol goes up, blood sugar levels rise,' warns Stephanie Driver, 'inflammation increases, blood becomes thicker and sticky, cancer cells spread more rapidly and the body becomes tired.'

Gradually cut down your intake over a week or so to minimise side effects. Keep a bottle of water on your desk or nearby and keep yourself well hydrated throughout the day – this also helps to raise energy levels. Try coffee substitutes and herbal and spiced teas. Don't be tempted to switch to decaff – sadly the decaffeination process uses distinctly unhealthy chemicals.

6. Save alcohol for the weekend

In the past, if I were overloaded or stressed, I would reach for the wine bottle at the end of the day like a drowning woman clutching a passing log. Unfortunately it's not an ideal way of de-stressing. Alcohol is a downer, so, although it does relax you, it can also make you maudlin or depressed, given long-term use. As with caffeine, it also affects sleep patterns, depriving you of the deep, restful sleep your body and mind need to recover (and remember that sleep is the only time our stress hormones knock off). Alcohol dulls your brain responses and, if you're not careful, will leave you under-functioning the next day.

Alcohol lowers your inhibitions so it's easy to polish off the whole bottle before you know it. While you're there, you'll be more prone to eating comfort food and vegging out in front of the television. Try breaking the habit. When you come home from work, change into comfortable clothes to signal you're no longer in work mode. Have a shower, do some stretches or yoga to wind you down in a more natural way. If you still crave a drink, concoct yourself an exotic non-alcoholic cocktail or smoothie that tastes special and that helps, rather than harms, your mind and body. Save alcohol for the weekend or special occasions – you will find you enjoy it far more if it isn't a regular occurrence. When you do drink, have two glasses of water for every alcoholic drink to keep your body adequately hydrated.

7. Limit your choices

I have found that limiting choices, across the board, makes life much easier and less stressful. That doesn't mean I don't buy nice things – but I am able to choose from a smaller range of nice things. I still go on holiday but I don't deluge myself with piles of brochures. Above all, I have learnt that it is time-consuming and stressful always to have to find the 'perfect' anything and that a 'pretty good' something will do just fine.

Seven rules for good choosing

1. Make your decisions non-reversible. Don't rely on the 'I can change this if I don't like it' dodge – whether it's a new handbag or a husband.

2. Don't let yourself dwell on how lovely the other choices (that you didn't choose) were. Let them go.

3. Don't regret the things/people/places/jobs you did – or didn't – choose. Wishing the past could be changed is pointless and makes you unhappy.

4. Control your expectations – recognise that the 'must-have' new bag or shoes, or whatever, won't change your life.

5. Anticipate 'adaptation' – the cruel rule of life that says that however much you adore something (or someone) when it's brand-new, your desire will dwindle and move from exhilaration into everyday acceptance (often very swiftly).

6. Don't compare what you choose with what others have or want. Look for what gives meaning to *your* life, not somebody else's.

7. Learn to love constraints. Choose from a smaller arena or variety. Find brands that work for you and stick with them (unless they fail you). Buy from smaller shops or a smaller range of shops or websites. Cast your net small – look for solutions locally – whether it's a partner, a home or a computer.

8. Cull your address book

We often continue doing the same things with the same people for years and years, long after we cease to derive any satisfaction from them. You are stuck with your family – no choices there. But where is it written in stone that you have to stick with the same friends, year in, year out? As we go through life, we change. Some friends will change and evolve in the same direction that you do – but very few will stay in tune throughout your whole life.

Friendships that are past their sell-by date create overload because they eat into time you could spend with people you actually like, whose company you enjoy, or from other activities. They also foster resentment (when you have to see them) or guilt (when you don't). Bottom line: with whom do you want to spend your time? Remember that a healthy friendship is based on give and take – you support each other. If you are always the full-time 'therapist' and you get no support in return, it's an unequal friendship and one that needs to go. Let's face it, in our overloaded society we have enough on our plates, without having to cope with everyone else's besides. Equally there are the so-called 'friends' who, overtly or subtly, put you down, make you feel bad about yourself. Who needs it? Dump them. There's no need to be cruel about it. All but the most persistent and thick-skinned people will fade away with benign neglect.

9. Create firm boundaries

Create specific cut-off points, boundaries, in your life. Vast numbers of us regularly bring work home, and, equally, take our home problems to work. If you can, separate the two again. If you are working productively, it should not be necessary to bring piles of work home. If this is impossible, you simply have too much work and need to address that issue. Talk to the person responsible for overloading your schedule and discuss what you can, and can't, do. If you're asked to take on something for which you know you don't have time, say firmly and politely, 'No.' Pacing yourself, eating elephants and planning large projects should mean that frantic last-minute dashes are a thing of the past. Remember that working beyond eight hours a day is usually counter-productive.

Leave the briefcase at work, your laptop unopened. Turn off your mobile. Turn on your voicemail (and be prepared to ignore it). Hunker down. You are not a worker ant (and you may be interested to know that worker ants work far fewer hours than the average executive). Discourage work calls at home. Equally, discourage social calls at work. When you are in each place your attention should stay focused on where you are and what you're doing. It will make you far more efficient at work, and far more relaxed and fun at home. Be honest: does the idea of being 'indispensable' make you feel good? If you're addicted to this myth, start to recognise it – it's the first step to overcoming it.

Wind down at the weekend

Another important boundary is that between the working week and the weekend. Most of us run as fast at the weekends as we do during the week. There is no pause button in modern life. Recognise that you will be able to do more, in the long run, if you sometimes do less. Any athlete will tell you that, in order to be able to sprint, you need to work steadily and rest frequently. Equally, when you go on holiday, *go* on holiday. Don't turn holidays into work in a different location. A laptop has no place in a beach bag.

10. Let go

The biggest change for the better you could make would be to drop the myth that doing it all is possible, or even desirable. Let go. Be honest about what you can – and can't – feasibly do in one day. Accept that if one area of your life is ruling the roost you cannot humanly expect to perform 100 per cent in the others. I know so many people who beat themselves up about their 'filthy' houses or their 'terrible' parenting when they are working regular 12-hour days. They honestly think they can cram all the other roles in their lives into four or five hours. No way.

Equally so many of us strive for permanent perfection. If we have a dinner party, it has to be exquisite; if we send a present it has to be the 'perfect' present. No, it doesn't. Your friends want to have a fun evening – they aren't going to be marking your table decorations out of ten and expecting Michelin-starred cuisine (and if they do, I'd suggest you have the wrong friends). The old adage 'it's the thought that counts' is true. I'm not saying become sloppy or slapdash – it's important to give thought and attention to what you do. However, you need to know when something is 'good enough' and be content to leave it there.

Chapter 8

Practical help for stressed workers

Why are so many of us heading for burnout? Why do so many people yearn to get out of the rat race and raise alpacas in the country? Because our work has lurched out of control, it has taken over our lives and bullied us into a state of total overload and misery.

We have already looked at many ways in which you can reduce your work overload – creating boundaries; controlling your mobile, the media and the Internet; putting aside the quest for perfection. In this chapter I'll look at some further ways of bringing work back to heel.

Coping with information overload

Let's face it; there is only so much information, only so many details that can be handled comfortably. According to Kevin A Miller, author of *Surviving Information Overload*, the world is now producing nearly two exabytes of new information a year. An exabyte is the equivalent of a billion gigabytes. By the time this book comes out that figure will probably be way too conservative. So, drop any idea of keeping up. The key to information overload is to be selective and smart about what you choose to take in.

It's also worth remembering that with so much information pouring out of every orifice of society, much of it is out of date within minutes or, frankly, wrong. I love this quote, attributed to a President of the Harvard Medical School, which goes, 'Fifty per cent of all we taught you is wrong. The trouble is, we don't know which fifty per cent.'

How do you get out of this tangle? Try these suggestions.

Top ten tips to curb information overload

1. You do not need to know everything all the time, just 'in case' you will need it in the future. Information changes so swiftly it is best to research as and when you need the material so that it isn't out of date. Einstein said, 'I make it a rule not to clutter my mind with simple information that I can find in a book in five minutes.' Do likewise.

2. Ignorance is not a sin. Ask yourself, 'Is there someone who is an expert on this?' Being the second to know about something can be incredibly useful. 'No, I didn't see that report. What did it say? Can you summarise?' Time saved.

3. Remember that the Internet doesn't always work and that human experts are often far better sources. A swift conversation with the right person could save hours.

4. Set strict criteria on what you decide to read and learn. Be honest. What is really necessary for your work? Do journals pile up on your desk? Is your inbox stuffed with on-line newsletters and updates? Be ruthless and unsubscribe to anything you do not regularly read and truly find useful.

5. Does it need to be *you* who reads this information? Could you delegate the reading of material to someone

else (you could then go to them for the information or ask for a short report of the content).

6. Cut down the frequency. Drop your daily newspaper in exchange for a weekly round up. Visit important websites once a month instead of every other day.

7. Purge electronic 'flatulence'. Is that email really necessary? Is it really necessary to cc it to so many people? Email can easily cause misunderstandings, and even offence – if it's a sensitive situation, don't use email. Think twice about sending that 'funny' joke or picture to everyone in your address book. Check virus alerts and 'please help' emails on websites such as www.hoax-slayer.com. Be suspicious of anything that says 'send to everyone you know.' Please do not *ever* forward chain letters.

8. Use a good spam filter and anti-virus software and run regular sweeps of your system to banish spyware, data-mining, scumware, tracking components, and so on. Keep a separate email account for purchasing on-line and always make sure you tick the box (or don't tick the box – read the small print carefully) to ensure your address won't be sold on. If (or rather *when*) you do get spam, don't click to 'unsubscribe' – it only confirms your address.

9. If you have a huge pile of publications waiting to be read, throw them away. Anything vital will certainly come up again in a future edition. The same goes for papers, notes, old statistics, and so on. If you're terrified of losing vital information, try deep-storing it (packed into boxes and dated). I always believe that if I haven't needed a piece of paper in three years I won't ever need it. Bin the boxes (unopened) on a regular basis.

10. Remember that over-stimulation equals overload.

Make your workplace a sanctuary

We have cottoned on to the idea that our homes should be sanctuaries – we buy scented candles, Buddha figures, plants and crystals as if there were a world shortage. But we haven't made the leap to the calm, serene workplace. Every office I ever worked in was poorly lit, messy, cluttered, noisy and stressful. Obviously a clean, clear workspace isn't going to take away your overload all by itself, but it will help you keep clear and focused.

1. If you suffer under fluorescent lighting, approach management about installing daylight bulbs.

2. Campaign for photocopiers, faxes and other electronic machinery to be put in a dedicated room (with good ventilation).

3. Clear all clutter. Get rid of all but vital files. Keep journals, papers, and so on, neatly filed away. Aim to operate a clear-desk policy.

4. Get fresh air. Air conditioning and central heating are to blame for the spread of colds and flu, and often give people 'sick office syndrome'. Have adequate ventilation and fresh air as much as possible.

5. Ensure your posture is good when working on screen or in manual jobs. Suggest the company employs a teacher of Alexander Technique to ensure nobody is putting unnecessary strain on their bodies (point out that this would save the company a fortune in days lost to backache – estimated at 180 million working days in the UK alone).

6. Have fresh flowers or plants in your office. If you work on-screen, have one or more of the 'anti-toxin' plants that have been proven (by NASA) to mop up EMFs (electromagnetic fields). Spider-plants, *scindapsus aureus* (golden pothos), *sansevieria* (mother-in-law's tongue) are all office super-plants.

7. If it's allowed, a candle on your desk focuses the mind and clears the air.

8. An enlightened office might go for a central aromatherapy burner, burning oils that promote calm, focused energy (or whatever mood your office requires). If not, you can have the same effect in a more subtle way by occasionally sniffing a tissue on to which you have put a few drops of your chosen oil. See below for the best anti-overload oils.

9. Try to make sure you do not have your back to a door – it will make you uneasy and stressed. If it's impossible to change your position, place a small mirror on your desk so you can see anyone approaching from behind. The ideal position for your desk is in the opposite corner to the door.

10. Don't crowd your desk with photos of your family, children, or even pets, as they will blur your boundaries. When at work, you need to have your whole attention on work (not home). Instead, have a team photo if it's not too cheesy, or inspiring images. A mandala is great because it can double-up as a meditation tool.

11. Whether you prefer working in serene silence or in the middle of a merry hubbub of voices or music is a personal choice. If you're out of sync with your fellow workers, explain to your boss and wear headphones – either to filter out unwanted voices or to plug in to your choice of music.

The anti-overload oils

Try these aromatherapy oils to keep stress levels low. Use a few drops in a burner or sprinkled on a tissue. Do not use neat on your skin.

You can also make up a blend of oils to use in the bath or for a massage. Simply add up to ten drops of oil (in total) to 30ml (2 tbsp) of sweet almond oil.

- **Clary sage** Good for tension, anxiety, low mood, depression, muscular tension, exhaustion, low libido. (CAUTION: do not take alcohol with clary sage – it causes nightmares.)

- **Geranium** Good for depression, anxiety, overexcitement, nervous tension, mood swings.
- **Lavender** Good for headaches, muscular tension, anxiety, depression, tension, insomnia, mood swings, restlessness.
- **Mandarin** Good for insomnia, nervous tension, restlessness, low mood.
- **Petitgrain** Good for nervous exhaustion, stress, insomnia.
- **Roman chamomile** Good for headaches, tension, anxiety, insomnia, irritability, muscular tension.
- **Sandalwood** Good for anxiety, nervousness, lack of confidence, depression, oversensitivity, fear, tiredness, low libido.
- **Ylang-ylang** Good for stress, shock, anxiety, anger, depression, nervousness, insomnia, tension, lack of confidence, low libido, sexual problems.

Good blends include clary sage, chamomile, lavender and geranium; or petitgrain, sandalwood and ylang-ylang. Or just experiment yourself.

Handling difficult people

By planning your days (and sticking to your plan) you should become far more efficient. Once you have organised yourself, however, you may still find you're overloaded at work. So you need to start looking at external factors – usually people. People can be too demanding, too needy, too bossy, too interfering – and all those qualities cause you stress.

Dealing with difficult people is a large topic but basically it all comes down to having strong self-esteem and self-confidence (we'll look at this in greater depth in Part Three). Most enlightened managers welcome self-assured workers and will understand that it is counter-productive for you to work inefficiently because you're overloaded. If your manager is a bully, he or she is probably (at heart) a coward – most bullies back right off if they are challenged. If yours doesn't, then it may be time to investigate a change of job. Statistics suggest that over half the workforce has been bullied at some point in his or her working life.

Alternatively, the problem could be that you have needy people around you, constantly unsure of themselves, always craving your time and approval. In this case, the best move is to boost their esteem where possible and yet also learn how to create clear boundaries. Many conflicts at work dig deep into our identity issues. Remember: you cannot ever control another person's response, but you can control your own. Prepare for difficult situations by imagining the other person responds in the most difficult manner possible, and ask yourself, 'What do I think this says about me?' Work through the identity issues in advance: is it OK for me to make someone cry? How will I respond? What if they attack my character or motivations? Then how would I respond? The more prepared you are for how the other person might react, the less surprised you'll be. Try to step back and think as if you were a mediator, a disinterested third party. Look at the situation from your viewpoint *and* the other person's viewpoint. Now take an overview and you will see that both of you simply have different views, different standards. So you could start the conversation by saying, 'You and I seem to have different ideas about [whatever]. Could we talk about it?' You can then both describe your stories and, hopefully, work out a compromise without either party feeling attacked.

Goodbye Mr/Ms Nice

However, the major lesson most overloaded people need to learn is how not to be so nice. Most of us are inherently nice – it's natural to want to make people feel good, and to want people to like you. But, while I'm not suggesting you should switch from nice to nasty, I do think most overloaded people could do with being firmer and franker. The following are good tips on how to deal with tricky people and – most importantly for your overload problem – how to say no.

1. Always give yourself time, a breathing space. Don't feel you have to respond immediately. Take a deep breath and think before you answer. Sometimes you can even say, 'I need to think about this. I'll be back in five minutes.'

2. Stand your ground – don't back off. Keep eye contact at all times. Don't allow people to invade your personal space – ask them to move back.

3. If you're tall, use your height. If you're smaller than the person you're dealing with, use space – keep a distance between you.

4. Get out your 'No!' immediately. Say 'No!' before anything else – then you can apologise all you like. You can even change your mind.

5. Always pay attention to how someone is responding to you rather than assuming their response. You cannot ever accurately guess what someone is thinking. Challenge your assumptions. Say, 'I assume you are thinking ...' Often you will find you are quite wrong.

6. Don't smile when you saying something serious. Most nice people dilute their point by smiling nervously.

7. If someone is arguing with you, take the wind out of their sails by agreeing with everything they say. The bombast has nowhere to go and then you can move on.

8. When you are in an argument with someone, try building bridges rather than just sticking to your agenda. Think, 'What can I give this person opposite me in order for things to change between us?' rather than 'What can I get from him/her?' This doesn't mean giving in; by offering something small in return you will often end up with your desired outcome.

Question presenteeism

Bottom line: do you need to be at work for all hours, or are you just expected to be? If this is the case, it might be worth telling your boss about the interesting case of Marriott, the large hotel chain. The powers that be at Marriott were concerned that their managers were suffering from lack of morale, disenchantment and burnout. The reason, they figured, was that they were staying late at the office for no real reason other than that they felt it was expected. So a pilot project was launched in which staff at a few hotels were told they should leave the office as soon as their work was done, regardless of the time on the clock. It took a little time but soon members of staff were openly leaving early. On average they worked five hours less per week. Did their work suffer? On the contrary – they are now far more productive.

This really shouldn't be a surprise. Productivity and optimum work-hours have been studied rigorously for nearly a century and every study has come to exactly the same conclusion: up to eight hour days, five days a week, offer maximum productivity. Go over that and productivity (in any industry you care to think of) starts to drop. The longer you work, the less you get done. Not only is it pointless in terms of productivity it's also dangerous for your health. Reducing your sleep by even one hour a night can result in a severe decrease in cognitive ability. Working over 21 hours continuously creates the same symptoms as being over the legal limit for alcohol – responses slow down, cognitive and motor skills deteriorate. The bottom line is that exhausted workers create errors.

If your workplace asks or expects you to be on-site beyond the normal working day, it is simply bad management. Let's stop this madness.

Road rage and commuting madness

Road rage is on the up. It's no wonder with our roads becoming ever more congested, parking spaces fewer and cars bigger. When you are stuck in your car, you have poor control and, as you will remember, control is a key factor to how we cope (or don't cope) with stress. If you are already overloaded, being stuck in a traffic jam or caught behind some idiot driving at 20mph could be the final straw.

Remember that you have a choice about how you react in every situation: you can choose to get worked up; you can choose to remain calm. It's safe to say that getting angry has never gotten anyone to work faster – but it has often resulted in fatal accidents.

The most valuable point to remember is that it's not personal. The person in front of you is not driving slowly just to wind you up. The nutter trying to overtake on the bend is not out to get you. Nobody knows who you are; they are just doing their own (albeit often stupid) thing. If you can't change or get out of a situation, the safest solution is to accept it. This applies, more than ever, with car scenarios. There is *nothing* (safe) you can do, so the most sensible course of action is to let go and accept what's happening.

With this in mind, it is a good idea to be prepared. Here's how:

....

Peaceful driving

Turn your car into your personal sanctuary, a pleasant stress-relieving comfort zone.

- Clear out all clutter: old newspapers, empty take-out cartons, coffee mugs, toys, sweet wrappers.
- Clean thoroughly (or have a valet) using natural products – a few drops of grapefruit essential oil on your duster is helpful.

- Choose music carefully to put you in the right frame of mind for driving – neither too aggressive nor too soporific.
- Or take the opportunity to 'read' a classic, or laugh with a favourite comedian via 'talking books'. Alternatively, listen to calming words of wisdom (but steer well clear of any CD that uses relaxation, self-hypnosis or visualisation techniques).
- Pack an 'anti-stress' emergency kit for if you get caught in a serious traffic jam: a good book; essential oils and tissues to put them on; healthy snacks; mineral water; cartoons to make you smile; photos of your loved ones.
- Essential oils for your car should be psychologically soothing while being physiologically stimulating. Good choices include bergamot, sweet orange, cypress, galbanum, lavender, geranium and pine.

If you get stuck in traffic, use your car as a portable sound therapy session – look at the suggestions in Chapter 18: The five extra secrets of a stress-free life.

Public transport can be a nightmare, too. Squashed on a crowded commuter train, or waiting in line for a bus or tube that doesn't come, is tedious and can send stress levels rising. Reframe the situation. Use this time – even if it's only for a few minutes – to practise stress-busting techniques. Not only will these help your immediate stress levels to subside but they will also help your overall stress responses:

Wu qi

This exercise comes from the Chinese mind-body system qi gong; it's both calming and energising, sending focused energy throughout the body.

1. Stand with your feet shoulder-width apart. Find your natural balance – your weight should neither be too far forward nor too far back.
2. Feel the rim of your foot, your heel, your little toe and big toe relaxed on the ground.
3. Keep your knees relaxed. Check your knees are exactly over your feet.
4. Relax your lower back. Relax your stomach and buttocks.
5. Let your chest become hollow. Relax and slightly round your shoulders.
6. Imagine you have a pigtail on top of your head, which is tied to a rafter on the roof. Let your head float lightly and freely. Relax your tongue, mouth and jaw.
7. Stay in this position with your hands hanging loosely by your sides.
8. Envisage a pure flame shimmering through your body, giving you energy.
9. When your transport arrives or you arrive at your destination, simply bring your awareness back to the world around you.

Commuter visualisation

This simple visualisation technique gives you a welcome amount of 'psychic space' and makes cramped commuting more bearable:

1. Breathe deeply for a few moments.
2. Now imagine a glow of bright white light deep in your heart.

3. As you breathe, it expands and becomes a shimmering white bubble, which grows and grows until it completely surrounds you.
4. If you wish, you can change the colour of your bubble – some people like a pure electric-blue, others a golden-pink. It's up to you.
5. Once you have practised this technique several times you will find you can call up your bubble in seconds – whenever you feel the need.

Crowd dancing

This is a great (and fun) exercise for making your way through crowded city streets and busy train stations. Your aim is to get to your destination without bumping into, or even touching, any other person.

1. Imagine you are dancing your way through the crowd. Look ahead and see your way through the crowd as if you were following a magic path. Be light on your feet, dodge into the gaps.
2. This is an exercise in total spatial awareness, intuition and control over your own body. Once you become expert, you can speed up until you really *are* almost dancing through the crowd.

Mindful walking

If you have a less hectic walk to work, you can actually use it to meditate. Whether it's a half-hour hike or a two-minute stroll, focusing on your footsteps becomes a mini-meditation, making you calm and focused for the day ahead.

1. Become aware of your walking. Walk slightly more slowly than normal and feel your feet touching the

ground (how does it feel?). Feel your toes spreading as you walk, be aware of your knees as they bend, your hips as they swing.

2. Now bring your attention to your breath. Mentally say 'in' as you inhale, and 'out' as you exhale.

3. See how many steps you take during each inhalation and how many during each exhalation. In your mind say, 'In – one, two, three, four' (or however many steps you take), and then, 'Out – one, two, three ...' Find your own rhythm.

4. Once you have become expert in this, you can spread your attention out around you, to notice the sounds, scents, sights around you. But keep coming back to the breath and the steps.

Chapter 9
The relationship MOT

This chapter is about how to save your relationship with your partner – and the other important relationships in your life. As we saw in Part One, when you're overloaded work usually runs roughshod over the rest of your life. The major casualties of overload's hit-and-run effect tend to be relationships. How many of these scenarios are all too familiar in your life?

- You'd planned to go out with friends but you end up working late in the office.
- It was your child's sports day/play/parent's evening but somehow you forgot to go (or left it to your partner).
- You used to have family holidays but now there just isn't time.
- You never seem to find time to sit down and talk to your partner, let alone go out together.
- You're far too tired for sex.
- You dread the sound of a friend on the phone – you don't have time to chat.

It's odd that, in our society, we seem to think it's quite OK to sideline the ones we love, to put our work before our family, to honour colleagues and ignore friends. Yes, work is important, but has it become *too* important in your life? It's time to think about your priorities and to make a deep commitment to the important people in your life.

Relationship circle

Start off by looking at the attention you give the people close to you in your life.

1. Write down a list of all the important people in your life.
2. Now, as you did in Chapter 5, draw a circle.
3. Divide it up according to how much true undivided attention you give to each person. Shocking? Probably. Ten to one you give more time to a co-worker than your own son or daughter.

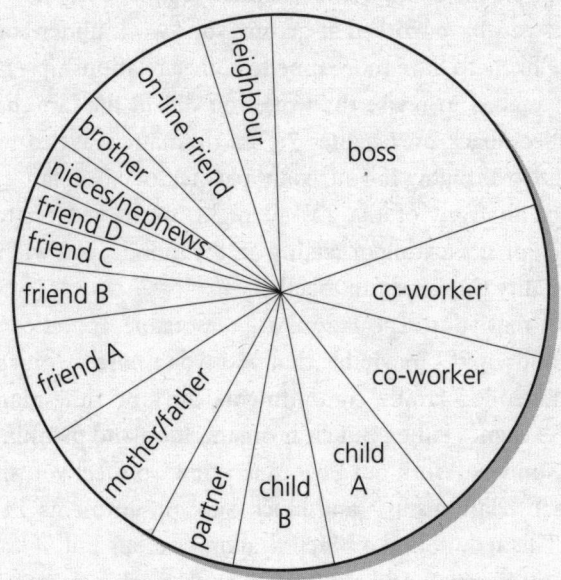

4. Draw another circle, this time with your ideal distribution of time to people.

I'm not saying that work relationships aren't important or that it's not valid to spend time talking to people at work – just be aware that we often give time freely at work, and baulk at giving it at home. Actually, the basic rules for clawing back relationships from the maw of overload are pretty similar to those we looked at in the last couple of chapters. Many couples and families operate in hopelessly disorganised ways and don't make the most of their limited time resources. So, first and foremost, go back to your planning sessions. Ensure that you are putting in enough time, not just for family and friends, but also for yourself. Many of us feel resentful of the demands of family life, of partners and friends, because we just don't have 'me-time'. If you have worked at getting your work under control, you are likely to have more time for other relationships. If not, you may need to revise the work you did in the last chapter. Also check back on Chapter 7: Ten dramatic ways to reduce overload overnight. If you, your partner or your family sits slumped in front of the TV all night, or logged on to the Internet, or sits texting or talking on the mobile, you will never have quality time and fun together.

Check that your expectations are reasonable. If you chose to have children, it's inevitable that you won't have as much free time. Extended family commitments can't be time-managed out of existence either. But clear organisation and planning can work wonders. Work out how much time you feel you should give each relationship – and block out 'appointments' in your diary. This may sound a bit clinical and callous but, if you are mired in overload and stuck in a work-work pattern, it can 'train' you back into balance.

What do you want from relationships?

When we are overloaded, we lose track of how to enjoy ourselves.

- Ask yourself what you want and hope for in each important relationship.
- What qualities and values are important in each relationship?
- What activities would you like to do with each important person?

Be very specific. It's not enough to say you want to 'have fun' with your children – what exactly would 'fun' comprise? If you want your partner to be 'loving' or 'sexy', how would 'loving' and 'sexy' translate into actions? The next step is really important. Sit down and talk to the people concerned, and find out what they think, what they would like, what qualities, values and activities are important to them. Sometimes you will find you have overlooked simple solutions. Parents might dutifully continue with activities that their children have long outgrown. Challenge your assumptions all the time. The basis for this is, of course, good communication, and that is our next topic.

Talk, talk, talk

All relationships thrive on clear communication. If you can't say what you think and feel, your relationship is basically on life support. Good communication takes time, effort and sheer hard work – for everyone. All relationships could do with a little soul-searching from time to time.

Inevitably you might disagree – whether you're debating with your partner, your six year old or your best friend. It's natural and quite healthy not always to be in total accord. Disagreements become toxic only when they degenerate into nasty rows. However, if you follow some simple 'good argument' guidelines, that should not occur.

The five keys to a good argument

1. Make sure you're both calm when you broach a tricky subject.
2. Talk in terms of your feelings and thoughts (i.e. 'I feel [upset, hurt, angry, insecure etc] about [specific action or statement by your partner]' rather than, 'You are a complete mean selfish bastard!' or similar.
3. Be specific, never general. For example, 'When you go off for the night with your mates without telling me, I feel hurt and worried' rather than, 'You just don't care about me – you're so selfish.'
4. Don't talk in codes; say what you really mean. For example, instead of 'Mike and your other workmates are just mindless idiots,' (which will make him leap to poor Mike's defence) try telling the truth: that you feel upset he's spending more time with Mike and his cronies than with you.
5. Suggest practical, specific solutions where possible. For example, 'How would it be if you saw Mike and the gang on Friday night while we go out on Thursdays?'

If you have children, make time to talk as a family. Sunday lunch is a good option – make it a ritual that you always sit down to a good meal and discuss 'family business'. This will take some getting used to, and careful handling, particularly if you have older children or teenagers. Involve them, don't talk down and don't hog the limelight. If one person does the lion's share of talking, have an ironically titled 'speaker's rod of power' (pepper-pot, serving spoon, Barbie, whatever) on the table.

Only the person with the 'rod' may talk and everyone else has to shut up and listen (really listen) until the 'rod' is put down. Find out what everyone wants from your family. Where are you going wrong? What are you doing right?

Getting the debate going

You could start the debate off by asking broad questions such as:

- What kind of home would you really like? Does our home fit the bill? If so, in which ways? If not, in which ways?
- What makes you want to come home? What keeps you away?
- Is there anything that is embarrassing about our family?
- What's the best thing about our family?

Ask yourselves what goals you could have as a family? How would you work towards them? Have everyone make a list of 50 things they would like to do as a family. This can range from very small one-off things (have a friend over to play, decorate a bedroom) to longer-term commitments (read a story together each night or play football in the park on Saturdays), to big joint ventures, however wistful or seemingly impossible (travel the world, move to the country, go to a different school).

Suggest to your family that they think of themselves as a team. What strengths and talents does each person have? Maybe assign tasks that call on those specific traits.

Above all, learn how to listen. Try to see the world through the other person's eyes, try to feel what they feel. You can do this by truly listening (not just biding time until you can put in your oar). Don't jump in and offer advice, just listen. Then reflect their comments back. For example, 'So, when you have to leave at eight o'clock you feel embarrassed in front of your friends?'

If you have got it right, the other person continues to explain; you continue to listen and reflect. If you don't understand the feelings, the other person puts you right. It's a tough exercise but very worthwhile.

If your partner or family refuse to communicate, or to even enter into discussions, you may need some expert help. See Resources for helpful organisations.

Creating solid partnerships

We take our partners for granted so much that, when overload takes control, many relationships just can't take the heat and they wither and die. However, simple checklists can fireproof your relationship and make it even stronger. The following are strategies that really work – practise some daily, some weekly, and some less frequently.

Daily

Pause before off-loading. Your relationship should be something that helps you both through the morass, not a further millstone round your necks. When you have had a tough day, give each other a few minutes. Have a hug, hang on tight and appreciate that here's someone nice after all the monsters at work/on the tube/on the roads ... and *then*, and *only* then, can you launch into the two-hour tirade against the world.

Start the day with a kiss. Try setting the alarm for just five minutes earlier and start your day with a kiss and a cuddle. Even if you are stuck miles apart you could always give each other a daily 'alarm call'. It takes only two minutes and starts the day on a happy note. Make time. A good rule of thumb is to take 15 to 20 minutes to talk *every day* in order to debrief, catch up, and say hello. That's all that is needed to keep most relationships healthy and on track. If you have children, you still need time alone.

Don't go to sleep on an argument. Clean up and hose down your relationship on a daily basis. Start each day afresh. Remind yourself what you love about your partner – and tell him or her. Appreciation, gratitude, thanks – *huge* defences against overload. More of this later in the book.

Oh, and touchy-feely stuff, too. Holding hands on the bus, cuddling up on the sofa, a lingering kiss. Loving touch is one sure-fire antidote to stress.

Once a week

Make one night special. Go to the cinema, for a walk in the country or out to eat. Or stay home and make time to give each other a massage or just talk.

Check out how you both feel. Successful couples spend time each week finding out exactly how each other is feeling, voicing anxieties, irritations and letting go of any resentment, fear or anger. Pick a time when you aren't rushed, or involved in other activities. Set aside time for sex; in a long-term relationship it's easy to give up on sex altogether. Make dates for sex and put them in your diary. Don't worry that you won't be 'in the mood' (if you waited until you were both 'in the mood' you might be in your graves). Anyhow, if you start off by just going through the motions, you will swiftly find that your body knows what to do and gets hot and bothered all by itself. Break away from the idea that sex has to be at a particular time or in a particular place – be inventive and willing to experiment. You might be pleasantly surprised.

Once a month

Share an adventure; shared interests and adventures help to bring you closer and give you something new in common. Widen your horizons and do something completely different. If you both fancy different things, make a list and take it in turns each month to try 'your' adventure.

Have an adventure – on your own. Time out gives you perspective, allows you to indulge in activities your partner doesn't like, and frees you from any resentment about the chore of daily life. Good relationships are strong and trusting enough for each of you to do your own thing from time to time.

Once a year

Assess your relationship; set aside time at least once a year to evaluate where you are as a couple. Ask, 'Which values do we share?', 'What is it we both want right now?', 'What is it we both want for the future?' Look at the current reality – what's working? What isn't? What do you appreciate or value about the other person? How well does the relationship meet your needs? Look at possibilities: if the relationship could be any way you wanted it to be, how would it be? What would it be different from the way things are right now? Take your time on this. Each of you should write down your answers to the questions above. Then discuss your answers with each other – you might be surprised.

Learn something new – together. It's an excuse to spend regular time together and gives you new interests (check it doesn't overload your schedules too far, however).

Fantasise: write a list of 100 things you each want to do in your life – from the mundane (get a haircut) to the extreme (travel around the world for a couple of years; change jobs; move to the country). Then read out your lists and compare your ideals. You may find some surprises, and possibly fantasies, in common that you could work towards turning into reality. You might find you both want to do less.

That sneaky perfectionism again

Just as perfectionism at work can lead to unnecessary overload, it can cause grief at home or with family and friends. When we demand that our relationships be perfect, we are setting ourselves up for disappointment and stress. This also applies to how we run our homes, how we plan our weekends and holidays, too. Yes, in an ideal world we would live in homes that are pristine and gorgeous – but the world isn't perfect. Yes, when you're overloaded and stressed out you crave the perfect holiday or weekend, but many of us don't allow ourselves to enjoy our time off because we fuss about the small details that aren't spot-on.

Face it: your partner won't ever be 100 per cent perfect. Your holiday will rarely be 100 per cent spot-on. But 80 per cent is pretty good, and 70 per cent isn't bad either. We need to loosen up a little, face the fact that we can say something totally vacuous, cook a soggy omelette or wear the wrong dress to the office party and still be accepted as part of the human race.

Ten remedies for relationships

A few final thoughts:

1. Resist the urge to criticise and complain; dish out compliments, not complaints.
2. If you're wrong, apologise. We all make mistakes – say sorry, and mean it.
3. Keep any promises, any dates, any appointments you make – faithfully.
4. Don't hold on to grudges and nurse grievances. Let go of the past.
5. Remember: relationships take work, hard work. Commit yourself fully to your relationship and be prepared to tough it out.

6. Think of things from your partner's/child's/friend's point of view. How would you see yourself through their eyes? Do you like what you see?

7. Think before you speak. Press your internal pause button before you say anything that could be hurtful.

8. Be honest – to yourself and to others.

9. Be flexible and open to change. Try new things with your family, partners and friends. Variety is the spice of life.

10. Remember the old adage: nobody looks back from their deathbed and wishes they had spent more time at the office.

Chapter 10

Moving away from money madness: the financial detox

Can money buy you happiness? No. Can it cause you stress? Yes. Will detoxing your finances help decrease overload? Absolutely.

The vast majority of us have been brought up to believe that if only we were rich enough we would be happy. It's a myth. Obviously if you're dirt poor, not having money is incredibly stressful. However, it's important to realise that the opposite is not true: when you have lots of money you do not lose stress. A study of US lottery winners a year after their wins revealed they were barely happier than the rest of us, despite possessing millions. A report by the World Values Survey concluded that our longing for money and material goods can actually be a 'happiness suppressant'. According to a survey by the Royal Economic Society, 'Even massive increases in wealth lead to only miniscule increases in happiness.' People whose incomes double report an increase in happiness of just 0.1 on a scale from one to ten. In Japan alone, individual wealth has increased by a thumping factor of five in the last 40 years, but – you've guessed it – with no measurable increase in the level of individual happiness.

Yet despite all this, still we cling to the conviction that if we only had enough money all our problems would vanish. As prosperity coach Lisa Wynn comments:

'It's staggering how many people blame money for their problems – and believe that if they had more, they would be happy. We are conditioned into thinking that having "more" makes us happy, so we work harder and harder to have more – and end up having less of a life as a result.'

Martin and Polly are a good case in point. Martin is a software designer and Polly is the vice-president of a large accounting firm. They have a large house, two cars, a 4×4 truck and a yacht. Are they contented? No way. They are two of the most stressed, irritable, discontented people I have ever met. They never have time to socialise, to hang out. They rarely even have time to use their boat. They are too busy working every hour to earn more money to buy the second home they now think will be the key to making them happy.

Here in the West we live in the most affluent society *ever*. We eat, drink and live better than kings and queens of the past – yet we aren't content. We want more. Once again, we suffer from comparing ourselves to other people, and – worst of all – to the celebrities we have turned into gods.

Sammy is 35, she is a successful executive in a record company, she earns a good salary and has a lovely apartment. She is also very beautiful. Yet Sammy is never satisfied. 'I must redo my apartment. I need an interior decorator. I must go to Prada and get something to wear

> for the Mercury Awards; and I need some Gina sandals to go with it. I need some liposuction. I wish I had longer legs. I'm getting worried I'm too old for my first facelift. God, I wish I could win the lottery.'

She's an extreme example, but most people do it to some degree. As we've seen, huge numbers of us are spiralling into debt, mainly because of our incapacity to deny ourselves anything at all. Meditation expert Richard Lawrence says:

The way to conquer debt is to conquer greed. Most of use money to buy things that we believe are going to improve the quality of our lives. But the truth is that our quality of life (providing we have all the basic material things we need) is not determined by how many TV channels we can watch or by how many shoes we have, it is determined by our inner state of mind. The person who experiences inner joy does not need most of the things that can get the materialist into debt.

So the first step to getting money madness under control is to stop and think, honestly and sincerely, about what would make you happy. If your knee-jerk reaction is still 'more money', try this exercise which is taken from Solution Therapy (also known as Solution Focused Therapy or Brief Therapy).

The Miracle Question

This is an insightful exercise that allows you to figure out exactly what you really need in your life. Give yourself plenty of time to do it. Sit down and ask yourself the following questions, or have someone else ask you:

1. If you woke up one morning and discovered that all your problems had disappeared overnight, how would you

know a miracle had happened? If your reaction would be to say something like, 'I would be rich,' or, 'I would discover I'd won the lottery,' try going beyond and looking at how you would actually feel.

2. How would you behave differently (be as precise as possible)? If you're still being woolly, keep going beyond. For example, if you answered, 'I'd be rich' you could continue with: how would you behave if you were rich? To which you might reply: 'I'd not have to work.' So then you would query: how would you feel if you didn't have to work? 'I'd be less stressed.' How would you know you were less stressed? 'I'd play with my children more. I'd go for walks. I'd talk to my partner …' Good practical strategies – that you could do right now. I hope you get the idea.

3. How would your family and friends behave differently?

4. How would *they* know a miracle had happened? How would *they* see the differences in your behaviour?

5. Are there parts of the miracle that are already happening in your life?

6. How have you got these things to happen? Can you get more of them to happen?

7. What elements of your life at present would you like to continue?

8. On a scale of nought to ten (where nought is the worst your life has been and ten is the day after the miracle), where are you now?

9. If you are on, say, four, how would you get to five? What would you be doing differently?

10. How would your family and friends know you had moved up one point?

The beauty of this exercise is that it shows the ideals and dreams that lie behind our yearning for money. Most people come out with interesting results. They find that their bottom line would be to spend more time with loved ones, to laugh more, to have fun, to feel a sense of peace and security. Others, when they're bravely honest, admit that they feel the need for more status, for admiration from other people. This is why they want the designer wardrobe, the perfect body, the massive house. When they break that down further they discover that they crave an increased sense of confidence and self-worth, or simply that they want love.

When you wish for money, remember that the rich are often the 'miserable rich'. They may earn huge salaries, live in vast houses and eat in fancy restaurants wearing stunning clothes, but they are either so overloaded they can barely enjoy them, or they feel a deep sense of emptiness inside that money can't plug. Try the Miracle Question and start bringing your own solutions into life. Change your behaviour and you will change your mind, no question.

Of course, this is deep stuff and we'll look into this issue in more depth in the next part of the book. But for now, just bear in mind your own bottom line: what is really important to you? Remind yourself that you can feel 'rich' in ways other than the materialistic. Find ways to be rich in love, happiness and fun. You could be rich in imagination, creativity, intelligence. You could be abundantly healthy, enjoying the feeling of a body that works well. Going beyond money and abundance means having your arms open to life, taking opportunities, revelling in being alive. Don't put off life until you 'have enough money' – find ways of exploring your dreams right now.

Take the time (I know, it's tough) to stop and examine your relationship with money. You might be surprised to find that it could have quite a deep emotional aspect. What are you really trying to buy? So many of us are trying to spend our way to what our hearts and souls desperately crave.

Linda, a PA, now recognises that, as the child of cold, frequently absent, parents, she felt very unloved and abandoned. When her parents came back from trips, they would give her expensive presents, and as Linda grew up she found an overwhelming urge to 'treat herself' as a way of loving herself. She saw it, at the time, as simply 'buying nice things to cheer me up'. Unfortunately she amassed huge debts on a clutch of credit cards and nearly lost her home. Once she realised where her craving was coming from, she was able to challenge it, understanding that spending was not the solution. She now recognises that what she really needs is not more Manolos, but a good relationship, and is having therapy and joining a dating agency.

Always be aware of the bottom line, what is *most* important in your life. Would you put your marriage on the line for the sake of a bigger house? Is promotion worth it, if you don't get to play with your children?

Your money programming

Some people save; some spend. What makes the difference? Often we learn our patterns around money extremely early on in our lives. If you want to get your finances straight, you need to investigate your early programming about money. Just as we pick up beliefs about life, love and expectations from our parents, carers and teachers, so we learn about money. Lisa Wynn often uses this exercise, which I find offers great insights:

You and money

1. Write down ten things your mother taught you about money.
2. Write down ten things your father taught you about money.
3. Look at other early messages you received about wealth, money and what you should or shouldn't expect.
4. Start tracing the roots of your beliefs about money and how they affected you – and then begin to challenge them.

You could have been taught, however unconsciously, that money brings happiness. Or that it's hard or impossible to get the money you need for security. How many of the following did you hear as a child? 'Money doesn't grow on trees.' 'Waste not, want not.' 'Diamonds are a girl's best friend.' 'It's tough to make ends meet.' 'There's never enough money.' 'Love doesn't last; money does.' Are those your beliefs now? Should they be? Remember that your subconscious mind will try to carry out what it thinks are your wishes, based on the messages you give yourself, consciously and subconsciously. Keep telling yourself, on some level, that 'there's never enough money' and, sure as eggs is eggs, there won't be. Isn't it time to change the way you think about money?

My family struggled desperately throughout my childhood to make ends meet. Fortunately my mother was a very creative, inventive and canny housekeeper and we got by. I grew up with the message that 'no matter what happens, you'll always survive' which has been incredibly useful. I don't have that terrible fear of falling through the cracks that many people do. However, I also picked up, 'We'll never be rich' and sure enough, I never have been. However, I have learnt that being rich is not the most important thing in my life, and that I can appreciate having 'enough' (and having the wisdom to know when there *is* 'enough'). I'm not saying 'money is bad' or that you shouldn't strive to be better off. Heaven's above, I'd take more cash with open arms. Affirmations can help here – bombarding your sub-conscious with positive phrases to beat that old negative conditioning. However, I'd suggest you keep your affirmations quite open. Rather than saying 'I deserve to be rich' or 'I choose to earn loads of money,' go for something like 'I now choose to be abundant in all areas of my life.' Or 'I have everything I need in my life, right now.'

The financial detox

So far, we've looked at some pretty esoteric stuff for a chapter about money. If you work on these areas, you will undoubtedly notice a change-around in your relationship to money – and may have some pleasant surprises. However, now it's time to look at the real nitty-gritty: practical ways to sort out your finances right now and stop them adding to your overload.

Start off by keeping a spending diary. Write down everything you spend, every last penny (and what you spend it on). If you have ever done a food diary, this is the same. You need to put down what you bought and how much it cost – and also (in the case of one-off purchases) the time you bought it and how you felt. So, for example:

1 pm (lunch time) feeling low. Tired. Bought dress (£45), shoes (£60), cappuccino and muffin (£4.50).

Do this for a month and don't cheat. Often this can be a real eye-opener as you realise where and why you are frittering money. At the end of the month, look back at your list with a critical eye. Highlight all non-essential purchases. Which of your purchases has brought you lasting pleasure or use, and which was a waste of money, a case of instant gratification? It can be useful to see in action just how often we think we 'need' something, when really we only 'want' it. The shoes that were so totally necessary to your existence – do they still hold that place in your affection?

Above all, add up how much you spent and compare it with your income. Are you living beyond your means? Are you relying on credit cards to keep you going from month to month? Don't. The major key to losing money overload is to live within your means. Here's how:

Ten steps to financial freedom

1. Commit to a budget. Work out how much you need for your essentials (mortgage/rent, insurance, bills, travel, food). Check to see if you can reduce your mortgage by switching to another provider – smart people switch regularly every few years to ensure the best deals (yet avoid penalties). Ensure you have the best possible rates from your utility suppliers – do some research and swap if necessary.

2. Pay off debts. Factor in as much as you can afford to pay off any debts. Negotiate with your creditors – if you stop your card and agree regular monthly payments, they may agree to cancel the interest. If your debts are huge it may be worth extending your mortgage term to pay off your debts – talk to your bank manager or independent financial adviser.

3. Curb your credit card. If you know you abuse your credit cards, be brutal and cut them up. If you are in debt, do *not* use credit cards until you are out of debt. Then use them only if you can pay them off in full each month.

4. What money do you have left? If possible, save a small amount (even if it's £10 a month). It gets you into a

good habit. If you still have some left, then, and only then, use it for small indulgences (but be aware of your spending and why you choose what you choose).

5. Always ask yourself, 'Do I need this or just want it?'

6. Find a 'money partner', someone who is better than you are with money to talk through your finances on a weekly basis. It doesn't need to be a professional – pick someone you admire for his or her sensible attitude to cash.

7. Make things last. Every time you find yourself lusting after the latest 'must-have', ask if it's really necessary. Think about mending or fixing rather than throwing away. It's much more eco-conscious, too, so you feel good about it.

8. Drop the labels. Are you buying status? Choose everything (from your clothes to where you eat) because of quality, rather than status. If you're addicted to labels, then check out the charity shops in the best districts – posh clothes for pennies.

9. Cut corners. Identify where you are wasting money and see if there are ways you could minimise wastage. For example, making your own sandwiches could save you hundreds of pounds a year. Take the bus instead of cabs. Switching to a smaller car could save you thousands on fuel, insurance and servicing.

10. Make the most of free things. Cutting the fancy gym membership and taking up jogging or swimming could save you thousands. Have a great day out at the park or in the country. Check out museums or art galleries that don't charge.

This sounds tough, and it is. But it is the only way of living overload-free from money. Don't go unconscious around money – own up to your spending and challenge your needs;

are they really wants? Remember that credit is simply spending money that isn't yours. Weigh up the instant gratification with the increased burden of debt. Is it worth the stress? Remember also that the feelgood moment is a very short-lived high. Review the advice on limiting choice in Chapter 7: Ten dramatic ways to reduce overload overnight – that will help, too.

Again, I am aware that I sound draconian. This is a plan for those of you that are in debt. If you are spending more than you earn, if you are using credit cards without paying them off in full each month, that's you. If you can say, hand on heart, that overspending doesn't cause you stress and contribute to your overload, then, fair enough (although I would say you were kidding yourself). Spending is an addiction, like any other. We become hooked on buying our latest 'fix'. Many people find that once they detox their finances their attitude to shopping totally changes. When you live without instant gratification, and find that your world doesn't fall apart, your thinking changes. You can still enjoy buying nice things, but it's not a compulsion. Often, even when you can afford them, you will pick things up and put them down, knowing that they will not really sustain your life. When this happens, you can start putting your savings into an account labelled 'round the world trip' or 're-training' or whatever would truly enhance your life. You can change your life in the long term, rather than giving yourself a short-term kick. Pull your finances into order, dump the 'quick fix' of the shopping hit, and you will be losing a huge chunk of overload – in a flash.

Chapter 11

The four super stress-reducers

Whatever the reasons for your overload, whatever your situation, there are four universal practices that will help with the stress overload causes. It's not a case of 'might help' or 'could help some people', they *will* help absolutely everyone. They won't, of themselves, cut out overload but what they will do is buffer you from many of the ill-effects of stress. How simple is simple? This simple: food, exercise, breathing, meditation. They are, of course, the cornerstones of a standard healthy lifestyle. In a sensible balanced world we would all be eating well, exercising adequately, breathing fully and deeply, and enjoying the health-boosting effects of regular meditation. But in this crazy muddled-up world, it's not a given. Maybe once again, the choice factor comes into play. We are bombarded with so much varying information that many of us simply give up trying to work out what we should be doing to stay healthy. Let's make it nice and simple.

Stress reducer #1: food

Fact: food affects mood. Fact: the food we choose can increase – or alleviate our stress response. Fact: poor food choices can create anxiety, hyperactivity and depression. There *is* such a thing as an anti-stress diet. Yet, curiously, huge numbers of us persist in eating what could be labelled the 'overload diet' – guaranteed to rev up your stress levels, increase anxiety, shunt you into depression and hopelessness. Naturopath Stephanie Driver says, 'I see an enormous number of people suffering from adrenal overload caused by stress, and also what I call food overload (in other words, weight problems).'

We use food as a reward or a bribe to children – offering chocolate to 'make it better', proffering sweets as a 'well done' at school, dishing out crisps to stop a temper tantrum in mid stream. No wonder, when we grow up, we turn to food in times of trouble, boredom or stress – our minds have come to rely on it as an emotional crutch. In a world packed with choice, in which the average Westerner is surrounded by mountains of food, the sad irony is that most people's diets are poor. I'm not saying you have to become a tofu-touting uber-vegan. I'm just saying that the links between the food we eat and the way we handle stress (and life in general) are indisputably linked. As nutritional therapist Patrick Holford says, so rightly, 'Instead of using pharmaceutical drugs with undesirable side effects, the medicine of tomorrow is food and supplements, to correct the body's chemistry and restore well-being.' I won't go into the science in huge depth (if you are interested, check out the books in the Bibliography) – but, briefly, we need to look at increasing foods that do the following:

1. Promote good brain chemistry – boosting levels of the feel-good chemicals, in particular the monoamine transporters: serotonin, dopamine and norepinephrine.
2. Support (rather than strain) the adrenal glands.
3. Keep blood-sugar levels balanced and even – so that you have a steady, focused level of energy.
4. Support your body at a cellular level – in the mitochondria where energy is made.

The anti-overload diet

Eat plenty of nourishing foods to give your body all the nutrients you need and cut out the harmful foods. The anti-overload diet is not intended to be a temporary fix but a new approach to eating that will help you throughout your life. It's not about denial but about re-education and enjoying the benefits of good eating.

Foods that nourish

Boost your diet with these foods, using organic wherever possible and, ideally, eat them when they are in season:

1. Whole grains (that is, brown rice, wild rice, barley, bulgur wheat, oats, millet, corn, quinoa) and whole-grain flour products (whole-wheat, rye, spelt and multiple-grain flours). NOTE: some people are intolerant of wheat or gluten – it can be worth testing for intolerances. Alternatively, try making your diet gluten-free for a month and see if any symptoms you are suffering from disappear.

2. Fresh vegetables. Pick a good mix of all types and all colours as they all have different benefits. For example, squashes and root vegetables are excellent serotonin boosters, whereas green, yellow and leafy vegetables have a neutral effect on brain chemistry but pack a hefty anti-oxidant punch.

3. Fresh fruit. Again, eat as wide a variety as you can manage. Make sure it's seasonal and naturally ripened to boost its essential glyconutrients.

4. Nuts and seeds. Packed with energy and beneficial fats, they make great snacks. NOTE: some people are allergic to nuts.

5. Pulses, legumes, beans and fermented soya bean products such as tofu and tempeh. NOTE: some people are intolerant of soya products.
6. Sprouted seeds, pulses and grains have massive amounts of micronutrients with immune-enhancing effects.
7. Lean (preferably organic) protein (chicken, turkey, fish, game).
8. Beneficial fats. Your body and brain need fat – but not all fats are created equal. Choose good quality hemp-seed oil, flaxseed oil, unrefined walnut oil, unrefined soybean oil for their optimum range and amount of essential fatty acids (EFAs). However, none of these can be heated. Cold-pressed extra virgin olive oil is rich in monounsaturates but low in EFAs – its value lies in the fact that it can be heated. Udo's Choice is recommended by many nutritional therapists and naturopaths as it is supremely high in EFAs – you will find it in most good health shops.

Foods that stress

Work on eliminating these from your diet (or cutting them right down):

- Caffeine (including tea, cola, chocolate).
- Alcohol.
- Sugar, and foods containing sugar.
- Refined carbohydrates (white flour, white pasta, pastry, and so on).
- Salt, and foods containing salt.
- Fat (other than those beneficial oils mentioned above). This includes butter, dairy products, meat products (other than lean protein mentioned before), hard fats (such as lard, margarine, meat fat), altered fats (such as

> hydrogenated vegetable fat found in nearly all processed food). Avoid deep-fried foods, too.
> * Processed foods, ready meals, fast food, 'junk' food – all of which contain high levels of fat, salt, sugar, artificial preservatives, colours and flavourings.
> * Diet foods – often contain artificial sweeteners and other additives that have unknown effects on our brains.

Wherever possible, avoid frying food. Instead try grilling, poaching, steaming, stewing – or eat vegetables raw. You can stir-fry foods without oil: simply use a non-stick pan and a little herb-flavoured stock in place of butter or oil.

Keeping salt intake low can be tough. You need a little (and I mean a little), but try to wean your taste buds off that salty taste. Instead, use herbs freely in your cooking. The optimum stress-busters are: basil, borage, chamomile, cinnamon, coriander (cilantro), ginger, lemon balm, marjoram, passionflower, peppermint. You can also drink many of them, either singly or combined, as tisanes (herbal teas).

Shift your diet slowly and don't inflict a totally draconian regime upon yourself.

Supplements

Should you take supplements? Opinion is fiercely divided. Those against say that if you eat a normal balanced diet you don't need supplements. Those in favour of taking supplements scoff that barely anyone eats an adequate diet and that supplements can fine-tune your body and mind. My view? I take supplements and do think they are valuable tools. However, I always consult a well-qualified nutritional therapist or naturopath rather than self-treating – and recommend you do, too. You *can* overdose and put your body out of balance. I asked

Stephanie Driver to recommend safe supplements to balance out an overloaded life:

- **Stress Advantage** by New Chapter – supports all your systems and organs during times of stress.
- **Vitamin B complex** (in particular B_5, B_6). Look for a supplement that includes 50–100 mg of each. Blackmores Executive B Stress Formula is designed specifically for stress and fatigue. This supplement also contains oats, which particularly nourish the adrenal glands.
- **Magnesium** A mineral vital for many enzyme reactions in the body is also essential for overloaded people. It is specific for the nervous system, helps muscles relax and improves energy. A dosage of 300 mg would be required to help. Take at night as it is better absorbed at this time and will help sleep as well.

In addition, Stephanie recommends the following herbs (in supplement form, rather than using in cooking):

- **Holy basil** lowers cortisol levels (which are elevated during chronic stress periods) and keeps the immune system strong. Promotes stamina and energy and improves performance.
- **Oats** (*Avena sativa*) 'feed' and balance the nervous system when under stress. Useful for over-stretched nerves, exhaustion and depression. Helps lower blood pressure, too.
- **Withania** (*Ashwagandha*) ayurvedic herb with powerful antioxidant, immune-enhancing and mind-soothing benefits.
- **Chamomile** calming to the central nervous system. Both German and Roman chamomile are gentle soothers. (CAUTION: chamomile interacts with warfarin and increases the action of sedative medication. Take separately from supplements containing iron, as chamomile decreases

absorption of iron).

- **Liquorice** a powerful adrenal support and immune-enhancing herb. It is profoundly energising and can also balance oestrogen levels. (CAUTION: do not use during pregnancy or if you have hypertension, kidney or liver disorders. Can increase blood pressure. Interacts with warfarin.)
- **Lemon balm** calming and sedative, lemon balm can help soothe anxiety and lift depression. Very gentle – you can also use essential oil of lemon balm in the bath or as a massage blend for stressed children.
- **Passionflower** helps irritability, nervous tension and feelings of hysteria. It's a sedative and mild narcotic, so useful for insomnia and that can't-relax-at-the-end-of-the-day feeling.
- **Siberian ginseng** A tonic adaptogenic herb. Helps to bring the body into balance, soothe the adrenals and boost the immune system. One of my personal favourites.

Stress reducer #2: exercise

Speeding up your body to slow down your mind may sound like a contradiction in terms, but exercise triggers the release of endorphins, the brain's natural mood improvers. Most importantly, exercise can prevent your body being stuck in a 'twilight zone' in which you are over-aroused through stress yet unable to disperse the stress hormones. Sports psychologist Christopher Connolly says, 'You need to kick yourself into a state of genuine physical arousal; by getting yourself into physical rather than mental arousal you can swing back into the state known as rest.' His prescription is good, hard training, solid aerobic or anaerobic exercise, which can give the full release that allows you to rest.

The key is to find a form of exercise you can enjoy. If you don't enjoy it, you won't stick with it. Think laterally. Which sports did you like when you were young? Is there anything you have always fancied trying? Schedule exercise into your diary – a solid appointment you don't skip. Squeeze in exercise on the way to or from work, or slide it into lunchtime. Just after work is ideal – but not later than 7 pm. If you have young children, it's tough, although more enlightened gyms and health clubs now provide crèches. Or, you could join up with a group of similarly overloaded friends or colleagues and provide an informal crèche for your kids.

Tough aerobic exercise provides the essential let-down of stress hormones, but many experts believe that soft meditative systems of exercise such as yoga, t'ai chi, qi gong or Pilates are more relaxing, and hence stress-relieving. A report in the *Lancet* claims that yoga relaxation exercises such as yoga nidra (a guided meditative technique) actually alter the neural networks of the brain, inducing deep rest.

It depends on your personality. If you find yoga too slow and irritating, better by far to lose yourself in a tough step class or circuit training. Once you have your stress more under control, or if you're a more laid-back person by nature, I'd certainly advise that you include yoga as part of your stress-busting package. My personal ideal is to include both the vigorous aerobic routines and also regular yoga. There really are no excuses. If you think you're too overloaded for exercise, try one of these:

- Install a mini trampoline (a rebounder) in front of your TV and bounce to the early morning news.
- Take a report or the latest 'must-read' publication to the gym and set it in front of your treadmill or static bike.
- Use work lunch hours (even if they are only 20 minutes) for some serious cardiovascular work, walking or running up and down the office stairs. But do warm up and stretch first.

- Combine your exercise with a social life. Meet friends or partners at the gym or go running, play squash, hike. A gang of you could take up a team sport.
- Spend family time getting active. Make sure the whole family is enjoying it and that you're not following only one person's dream.

Stress reducer # 3: breathing

Few of us realise that good breathing is an art, a science, a profound and effective way of boosting our health, altering our mood and shifting our stress response. Research reported in the *International Journal of Neuroscience* indicates that the ancient yogis were right in claiming that yogic breathing techniques, such as breathing through one nostril at a time, can affect a huge range of bodily responses, from cardiovascular activity to hormone balance, to shifts in the nervous system, all of which affect our ability to deal with stress.

Followers of Eastern practices such as yoga and qi gong say that breathing fully feeds the brain, calms the nerves and has a measurable effect on a number of medical conditions, lowering heart and metabolic rate; normalising blood pressure and decreasing the risks of cardiovascular disease. In other words it can counteract many of the ill-effects of stress and overload. There are very simple exercises that can help our breathing. The yogic tradition of India developed a whole science of good breathing. It is called *pranyama*, the science of breath control and expansion. Here's just one technique to get you started.

The complete breath

This encourages you to breathe fully, bringing oxygen deep into the cells. It's easiest to learn it lying down (so you can observe what's going on). Once learnt, you can practise any time, anywhere – the more frequently, the better. Start small and build up your practice. At first you may only manage a few breaths – that's fine. Don't ever strain your breathing and if, at any time, you feel uncomfortable, stop and breathe normally.

1. Lie down comfortably on the floor. Bring your feet close in to your buttocks and allow the feet to fall apart, bringing the soles of the feet together, hands resting gently on your abdomen. (Note: this may feel uncomfortable and, if so, you can put cushions under your knees.) This posture stretches the lower abdomen, which enhances the breathing process.

2. Breathe in with a slow, smooth inhalation through your nostrils, feeling your abdomen expand and contract. Your fingers will part as your abdomen expands.

3. Exhale slowly and steadily through your nostrils, noticing your abdomen flatten and that your fingers are once again touching.

4. Pause for a second or two and then repeat this inhalation and exhalation, becoming conscious of the movement of the breath down through your chest and abdomen. Breathe naturally at your own pace in this way for around five minutes or as long as you feel comfortable.

5. If you feel happy with this you can extend the breath so that it comes up from the abdomen into the chest as you inhale. This provides a longer, deeper breath.

6. Finally, bring your knees together and gently stretch out the legs. Allow yourself to relax on the floor for a few minutes (you may feel more comfortable with a cushion under your lower back or your neck).

Stress reducer # 4: meditation

Researchers have found that meditation can reduce hypertension, serum cholesterol and blood cortisol, all of which are related to stress in the body. Anxiety, depression and irritability all decrease while memory improves and reaction times become faster. A surprising number of politicians and business people claim meditation is the key to their success, enabling them to deal with high levels of stress without succumbing to overload.

Meditation could even save you hours each day. Research shows that meditation helps you focus, concentrate and generally think more clearly throughout the day. It also improves decision-making and increases stamina.

There's really nothing mysterious about meditation. You simply sit (on the floor or on a straight-backed chair). Now bring your attention to your breathing. Don't *try* to do anything, just watch your breathing. If thoughts arise, acknowledge them, and then let them go. The art is to notice your thoughts but not become attached to them and lose yourself, following wherever your mind wants to wander. Some people like to close their eyes, others find it easier to focus on a candle flame, or a mandala. Sounds can be used as a focus, too – the most familiar is the mantra *Ohm*. As with breathing, start small. Five minutes is usually enough for beginner meditators. Gradually you will find you can extend your practice. The optimum is 45 minutes twice a day, but whatever you can manage will be fine. It's more important to meditate for a short period regularly, then go for long protracted sessions every once in a while.

Sue Weston, who teaches anger management and relaxation, suggests an effective form for busy minds. You simply count from one to ten, becoming totally aware of each number. If other thoughts pop into your head, you simply start back again at one. She says that if you manage to get past five, you're a rare person.

Mindfulness, a close cousin to meditation, doesn't even require dedicated practice. Simply have times throughout the day when you become aware of where you are, what you're doing and feeling. Sit, breathe, and notice how your body feels. You can practise mindful eating, mindful walking (as we discussed in Chapter 8: Practical help for stressed workers), mindful showering. Just spend two or three minutes getting in touch with yourself and your body and mind.

David Harp, author of *The 3-Minute Meditator*, suggests countless ways of bringing meditation and mindfulness into everyday life. Try these:

The chore-based breath count

Practise this in conjunction with a specific task or chore that you do on a daily basis (for example, pouring a glass of water, putting paper into the printer). Simply count the number of breaths it takes you to do the task (number each exhale and don't try to control the speed). If your thoughts intrude, let them go, focus on your 'task', which is getting an accurate count of your breaths.

Tongue-block breath meditation

This comes from Kriya yoga and helps to emphasise attention on the breath. Simply touch the tip of your tongue to the roof of your mouth, less than an inch behind your upper front teeth. As you inhale you'll feel the coolness of each breath on the underside of your tongue.

Part Three

The Solution to Banish Overload Forever

Chapter 12

Preparing for change

By now, hopefully, you will have learnt useful ways of cutting back your overload. In this final section of the book, we're going to go much deeper. We're going to look at how it is possible to cut overload entirely from your life. Yes, it really *is* possible. However, it does call for a radical shift in the way you think, the way you define yourself and the way you choose to live your life.

It's far more subtle work than we have covered in the last section. It's about shifting your attitude, and looking deep inside. I suppose, in a very real sense, it's 'soul work' and so it won't be to everyone's taste. However, I would suggest that, even if you baulk at the idea, you at least try to read these suggestions with an open mind. You may not be ready for this path right now, but I'd like you to realise that there are ways out, there *are* options you can take – if not now then possibly in the future. That way, you need never feel trapped and penned in by overload – you will always know you can step off the treadmill, at any time.

Creating a space

Before we launch into the work proper, I think it's important to do some preparatory work. When you're overloaded, it can become impossible to see the wood for the trees. You're so busy, so stressed, that you find it tough to make good, life-affirming decisions. If you possibly can, try to get away or at least take some time out from your regular schedule, before you contemplate any major life shift. Take yourself off by yourself (if possible) to somewhere quiet and contemplative (it could even be somewhere glamorous, but make sure you won't be too distracted). Take this book with you and do the exercises in peace. Elaine St James, author of several wonderful books on simplifying your life, said that when she made the decision to cut out overload, she took a four-day break in a local retreat house. She says it took a couple of days before she could calm down and unwind enough to think clearly about her life and what she wanted.

If you have children or other dependants, of course this becomes harder. But I still think it's possible to get away for a weekend (if you can't, then you need to work on those support systems we discussed in the last part of the book, or have a firm word with your partner). It need not be expensive either – many retreat centres offer very reasonable rates. It doesn't even have to be a dedicated retreat space – you could ask a friend if you could use his or her home during the day while they're away at work. If push comes to shove, you can do it at home – but it can be tough to focus surrounded by everyday stuff and your 'old' lifestyle. Clear a space for your work. You will need to find somewhere you can be on your own and not cluttered. Props are not essential, but a candle always helps to focus attention and it clears the air. Try burning some of the aromatherapy oils discussed in Chapter 8: Practical help for stressed workers, to provide a soothing background.

Healing negative emotions

First and foremost, review the last chapter and commit to practising some form of meditation every day. This is particularly important if you are trying to make changes while living your everyday life. If you don't have a physical sanctuary or retreat space, you can at least make clear space in your head for a mental retreat.

Next, I would suggest you take some Bach flower remedies. The Bach remedies work to shift negative emotional patterns and so are invaluable when preparing to work on overload. The ones that follow are, to my mind, often the most useful for stressed, overloaded people:

....

The top ten Bach flower remedies for overloaded people

1. **Centaury** You're the archetypal doormat who can never say no. You always give more than you have the energy to give and usually find people take huge advantage of your generosity. Self-esteem can be a big issue for you.

2. **Hornbeam** You're overloaded, exhausted and feel you have no strength left to cope (although this is mainly in the mind). You have that typical 'Monday morning' feeling and need coffee to get you going. You suffer easily from information overload. Your lifestyle is far too sedentary for your own good.

3. **Impatiens** You are tense and suffer from frustration when things don't go fast enough. You live at a fast pace and find it hard to delegate, as it's always quicker to do tasks yourself. You can easily be addicted to your mobile, the Internet, coffee, drugs, anything that makes life faster.

4. **Oak** You're a strong, dependable person who is prone to overwork. You will fight against all the odds and never give up. You will willingly help others, even when you're exhausted. You can get totally worn out yet never complain. Instead you become depressed and despondent.

5. **Olive** You have become completely exhausted following a long period of intense strain. Everything in life has become a huge effort. You are suffering from intense physical, mental and spiritual fatigue, a deep inner tiredness that nothing relieves. This is a great remedy for burnout.

6. **Rock water** You are a total perfectionist and set yourself impossible standards. You are very tough on yourself, always berating yourself and forcing yourself to do more.

7. **Scleranthus** Your moods fluctuate wildly and your thoughts are erratic. You find it virtually impossible to make any kind of decision. This remedy often helps in cases of burnout and breakdown.

8. **Sweet chestnut** You feel you are at your wits' end, that you have reached the very limits of your endurance. You feel you have your back to the wall and are petrified of breaking down under the stress. A remedy for extreme despair and dejection.

9. **Vervain** You are intense, highly strung, over-enthusiastic and fanatical about causes close to your heart. You live on your nerves and keep yourself going with emotional energy. You are hugely prone to overwork and give 150 per cent of yourself to any task. You can't let go.

10. **White chestnut** You are anxious, often over-tired and depressed. This is your remedy if you regularly lie in bed, unable to sleep, with thoughts buzzing round and round your head. You worry away at problems but get nowhere.

Choose up to five remedies to work with at any one time. Buy a stock bottle (a small glass bottle) from a chemist and fill it about two-thirds full with spring water. Add 5ml (1 teaspoon) of brandy or cider vinegar for preservation. Now add two drops each of your chosen remedies. Shake the bottle to mix. Take four drops in water four times a day – when you wake, before lunch (on an empty stomach), around 5 pm (on an empty stomach) and just before you go to sleep. The remedies can help put you on a more level playing field. They can gently reframe any addictive behaviour and negative thought patterns that contribute to overload.

Starting the work

Before you start, just take a moment to remind yourself how hard you have been working, and how well you have done to have kept going as long as you have. Recognise that life is not fair and can be very tough. Accept that it isn't 'your fault' necessarily, but the way society is set up. Give yourself a pat on the back for coping as well as you have, or some sincere sympathy for not coping. In other words, stop beating yourself up for a change.

Next, look long and hard at your overload and work out precisely what it's costing you. What is the real problem with your life as you're living it right now? If you want to change your life you need to have very clear, focused motivation. Ask yourself these questions:

1. Am I damaging my relationship? Am I wrecking even the chance of *having* a relationship?
2. Am I damaging my relationship with my children? Or am I risking the chance of ever *having* children?
3. Am I damaging my health, my fitness, my well-being? Am I possibly shortening my life or putting myself at risk of serious illness?
4. Am I cutting myself off from my family and the wider community? Am I missing out?
5. Am I threatening my financial stability? Is my overload making me spend more? Is my spending keeping me overloaded?
6. Am I sidelining my creativity, my sense of fun, my very soul?

Recognising what you are missing by continuing with your overloaded life can be a powerful motivator for change, so do spend some time with this. Review the exercises in Chapter 5: The fork in the crossroads – or do them now if you haven't already gone through them. Ask yourself the vital question:

Why do I *choose* to be overloaded?

Ask yourself, truthfully, whether you may be overloaded because you are frightened. Would you prefer to be too busy than to have the time to stop and have to think about life? What would you do with your spare time if you did have some? Many people panic at the thought, fearing loneliness or boredom, or inertia. For them, working, and even overworking, is better than a blank gap.

> *Jason*, a TV researcher, readily admits that this is the main reason for his overload. 'I work late because I don't want to go home to an empty house. When I do have time off, I don't know what to do with it. I just flick through Sky or play computer games, or go to bed early.'

Of course, it's not just work that can keep you busy. Do you race from one social appointment to the next, or volunteer for good works, or obsessively clean the house, because you are terrified of a void that would require you to stop and analyse your life?

> *Dora* is a classic example. A widow in her late fifties, her children have grown up and left home. Dora never stops. She runs a B&B, helps out in a charity shop, drives disabled people, walks dogs and belongs to a host of societies and clubs. She plans her life down to the last minute and panics if she has a spare hour. Dora complains she is overloaded but it's clear to everyone, except her, that she is terrified of being alone.

If you recognise yourself in Jason or Dora, I would suggest that it is vitally important for you to work with the material in this part of the book. Or maybe think about working one-to-one with a good psychotherapist, of the more spiritual kind – I would suggest transpersonal psychotherapy, Jungian psychotherapy, Gestalt therapy or Process (Process Orientated Psychology) work. Review your answers to the Miracle Question in Chapter 10: Moving away from money madness. Again, if you did not do it then (perhaps money wasn't an issue for you) do try it now. It really can help you get to the bottom of what you really *really* want and need in your life.

Treasure mapping

I have been using treasure maps for 20 years now – I have one on my office wall right now as I type this. Basically they are a way of accessing your subconscious mind. They work because the subconscious understands images and symbols much better than it understands words (hence dreams won't spell out an answer in literal form but will show it symbolically). By making a treasure map you're allowing your subconscious to give you strong hints about what you really need in your life. It works like this:

1. Get together a stack of old magazines – the wider the selection the better.
2. Browse through, snipping out any images that appeal to you. Try not to think about it too much. Don't worry if they seem ridiculous, or impossible or selfish. Feel free to snip out huge houses, or fancy cars, or gorgeous clothes if they truly call. You could find yourself drawn to more general images – people having fun, relaxing, playing with children or animals. They might even be quite abstract – colours, or shapes. It doesn't matter.
3. Now put your pile of clippings aside for about a week.

4. This time go through them and pull out those that are your absolute favourites. You will be putting them on a large sheet of paper – anything up to about 90 centimetres (3 feet) square – so you can have a good choice. But ensure that each one really gives you a tingle down your spine.

5. Stick those images on to the paper. You can also include a photograph of yourself and any phrases that ring true. Poetry or quotations are fine, too. Now, put the 'map' where you will see it on a regular basis – opposite your desk, or in the kitchen for example.

6. If at any time an image doesn't ring true, take it off.

This will help to clarify what your subconscious really craves. Often it can come up with surprising material. For instance, when I did a treasure map to ascertain what kind of house I should be seeking, I was surprised to find I kept coming up with pictures of babies (a few months later I was pregnant). The additional bonus is that, having put out your subconscious desires in such graphic form, your subconscious will try to make them come true, often in surprising ways. I know people who have been able to change job, start businesses, start families, downshift, upshift, whatever – all through treasure mapping. Above all, it can help clarify what you need in your life. Elaine St James says that a staggering 65 per cent of people spend the small amount of leisure time they have doing things they don't want to do. Amazing, but true. So do try the treasure map; you might be surprised at what happens.

What do you want from life?

Look at your treasure map, your answers to the Miracle Question and think about what your life would look like if you weren't overloaded. It will be very different for everyone. There is no one right answer. You might want to:

- Simply reduce the stress levels in your life.
- Eliminate rushing, hurrying, trying to be in two places at once.
- Have enough energy to enjoy your partner, your family.
- Investigate other ways of earning a living, or of working in a different way.
- Have more challenges in your life; have more friends or activities (some people are stressed because they are *under*-stimulated, not over-stimulated).
- Make room for a big life change – having a baby, starting a business, travelling, being creative.

Rest assured, you won't be alone in wanting to re-evaluate and rethink your life. A *Fortune* magazine poll of 20-something Americans found that a staggering 75 per cent were 'more concerned with a rich family or spiritual life, a rewarding job, the chance to help others, and the opportunity for leisure and travel or for intellectual and creative enrichment' than they were for wealth. What stops us? Time to look at the major deep-level cause of overload – our ego.

Chapter 13
Ego, self-esteem, the Self and the soul

I firmly believe that if you truly want to overcome overload you have to look at your ego. The ego is an essential part of our psyche – but (and this is important) it is only *one part* of our psyche. The ego is the way we identify ourselves; it says, 'I am this kind of person, not that kind of person.' It's about our values, our beliefs; it sets us apart from other people and fosters our sense of uniqueness. A well-developed 'healthy' ego is vital for everyday life because it gives us a firm sense of self-esteem, self-respect, independence and individuality. People with healthy, balanced egos rarely suffer from crippling overload. They may get stressed, but usually they have the ability to say no; they refuse to take on too much, they simply won't juggle impossible loads.

The need for a strong ego

Many spiritual teachers teach that we should attempt to banish ego entirely, to transcend it. The reasoning is that ego distracts us from spirituality, that it is greedy and even evil. That is pretty unrealistic, and frankly untrue. The problem is not *having* an ego, but having an unbalanced or undeveloped ego, an unhealthy ego.

'I'm all for ego. We all need good strong egos,' says psychotherapist Sarah Dening, 'At some point, particularly in later life, you might try to transcend the ego, but you have to have a strong ego in the first place or the world will just swamp you.'

When you don't have a strong sense of ego, it's easy to become arrogant, pompous and conceited, in an attempt to compensate for lack of self-esteem. You can become seduced by status, lured by possessions and wealth, caught up in the hell of expectation and workaholism because your fragile ego will push you to seek approval from the outside world rather than from a deep-seated sense of inner worth. If you live at the mercy of a weak ego, you will find yourself compulsively craving 'ego-gratification', striving for possessions and titles that appear to give you power, recognition, success and applause. You will look to externals to make you feel more complete, better about yourself.

People with weak egos have poor boundaries – fatal if you are trying to overcome overload. Boundaries are a large part of the overload equation. If you don't have your boundaries set firmly in place, you will inevitably get yourself in a mess in today's harsh, brutal world. It's essential to be able to say, 'That's my limit. I will do this, but not that. I will go this far but no further.'

What are your beliefs?

Every time you are faced with a situation there are some vital questions you must ask yourself:

1. What is in this for me?
2. What is my responsibility in this situation – to myself and to the other people involved?
3. Does it make sense for me to sacrifice myself in this given situation?

'It sounds selfish, but it's imperative,' says Sarah:

You have to know why you're doing what you're doing. The more
you are aware of your motivation for your actions, the more self-
esteem you will have, because you will have taken responsibility,
honoured yourself and honoured the other person or people.
There are no hard-and-fast rules in this because only an individual can decide their own value system, but the important thing is
to know one, and to have one.

Do you know your values? Not necessarily. It's not something
we're taught to dwell on in our society.

Think about what constitutes your ego, or what *should* con-
stitute it.

- What are *your* values?
- What are *your* beliefs?
- What do *you* think is really important in life?

I'm emphasising the *you* bits because so many people without
strong egos will take on board the beliefs and views and values
of other, stronger people. Check it out:

- Which of 'your' beliefs don't ring true?
- Which might belong to other people?

Isn't it now time to be your own person with your own sense
of identity?

Janice is a good example of someone with poor ego
boundaries. Unsure of exactly who she is, Janice lives her
life vicariously through various soap stars and pop singers.
She trawls through celebrity magazines, poring over these
women's likes and dislikes, pouncing on their advice and
fashion style. She will happily spend huge amounts of her

salary on the latest handbag or shoes, if one of her idols endorses it. She has no values of her own, and constantly takes on board those of other, seemingly successful, people. Harriet is similar. She doesn't feel complete unless she portrays a perfect image – running up huge debts buying designer wardrobes each season, to 'look the part'. If her ego were stronger, she simply wouldn't have the terrible need to 'look right' – because she would 'feel right' inside.

The role of the persona

Of course, you may need a certain amount of smart 'stuff' to embellish your work persona. The persona is the image we present to the world, how other people see us. Sarah Dening says:

> Everyone needs a persona because you can't really present yourself as you are to the world, lock, stock and barrel. You have to protect yourself a bit. Plus, if you want to get into the social swim, there are times you have to put on a nice friendly face, or you may need a professional persona. You can put on your persona, like a set of clothes, in the morning. However, remember that if this isn't how you really are, you need to be able to take off that persona when you get home.

Again, it comes down to boundaries.

Have you learnt how to turn your persona on and off as required? Are you still being the pompous businessman when you're playing with your children?

Conversely, are you still being the people-pleaser when you walk into work and need to ask for a pay rise?

So persona is all about image – the word 'persona' refers to the mask actors from ancient Greece would wear to show the role they were playing (smiling face for comedy, sad face for tragedy, and so on). Ego, on the other hand, is about your own sense of Self.

Gaining perspective

The ego's job is to protect us. It's a bit like an over-enthusiastic financial adviser who would like to sell us every policy and savings plan going. But, just as you wouldn't subscribe to every single policy and plan, you don't have to take on board every one of the ego's demands. You can pick and choose. Yes, you need a warm, strong, comfortable home that is big enough for your needs. No, you don't need a bloated house that will echo with empty space and wreck your finances. Yes, of course it's good to have a great job that pays well and in which you are respected. But should you put up with overload or bullying because of the status it bestows? Keep perspective. Simply by recognising that your ego is not the entire *you* is helpful.

Negotiate with your ego – yes it is possible.

Use the 'two chairs' technique from Gestalt therapy. Set up two chairs facing each other. Sit on one chair as your 'Self'; imagine your ego self is sitting on the other. Now talk to your ego. For example, 'Why do you want to go for that promotion?' Now move over to the 'ego' chair and answer from your ego's perspective: 'Because it would give more security. We'd look better. We'd have more money.'

Now move back (from Self's perspective): 'But it would take more time and be less pleasant work. How about if we just ask for a pay rise?' Recognise that it is your insecure ego that seeks overload – that pushes you to be 'the best', 'the busiest', that chivvies you into anxiety about not being on call 24/7, that panics that you won't have a job if you don't give it every last ounce of your energy. Become wise. Start to recognise that things, however lovely, will never give you a true identity. They may momentarily boost a fragile ego, but they will not *ever* satisfy the deep yearnings of the soul. If you always listen to an insecure ego and pursue this course, you will *never* have enough, your house will never be expensive or grand enough, you will never have a good enough job.

Self-esteem: the healthy ego

Weak ego and low self-esteem go hand in hand. When you don't have a strong ego, your self-esteem goes into free fall. It acts like a brake on everything you do. While ego is about our values and beliefs, self-esteem is about how good we feel about ourselves. Poor self-esteem is the voice in your mind that says, 'You can't do that because you're not good enough.' It tries to protect you but, like an overprotective mother wrapping her child in cotton wool, it prevents you from getting out there and enjoying life and all it has to offer.

Our self-esteem quota often dates right back to impressions we absorbed as children. The messages we picked up from parents, teachers and peers get lodged in the subconscious, grabbed upon by the ego, and can affect everything from body image through social adeptness to self-confidence at work. If you have good self-esteem you will be able to say 'no' firmly and clearly; you will be able to build clear boundaries and stick to them. These exercises work directly with your self-esteem, helping you gain perspective.

1. Map out your life

Sit down with a large pad and mark each page with a different category: your appearance; your personality; your work; your home life; your relationships; your sex life; and your social life. On one side of the page make a list of all your virtues and strengths. On the other side list your bad points and weaknesses.

1. Which list is longest and where are all the negative answers clustered? This will focus on those areas that need attention.

2. Are your, or other people's, criticisms really valid or accurate? Replace words like 'stupid' with something more accurate like 'I panic when I have to talk in public' or 'I am sometimes a bit forgetful.'

3. Are all your criticisms still valid? Often we hang on to labels long after we have moved on from that kind of behaviour. Are you still beating yourself up for the way you were when you were a child or adolescent? Maybe you were a shy, awkward teenager – but are you truly still that person?

4. Take particular notice of your good points – write a list and stick it on the bathroom mirror or inside your wardrobe and read it and add to it every day. For example: 'I am generous, open-hearted, a good friend, smart, imaginative, creative, sexy and I have gorgeous feet!'

2. Banish the inner critic

Listen to the little ego voice that constantly comments on your behaviour – the censor that says, 'You're a fat lump,' or 'You're not good enough.' The critic is a part of our brain that often links us to early authority figures such as parents and teachers.

1. Try to recognise the voice. Does it sound like anyone you know? Often it can come from a parent, sibling, relative, teacher, friend, sports coach. Naming your critic is half the battle.

2. Keep a thought diary and write down every negative thought you have. At the end of each day, look at your list

and work out the purpose behind each thought – was it goading you to do better or was it giving you an excuse for not doing as well as you might?

3. Start getting angry with your inner critic and silently shout at it every time it starts to attack. 'Shut up!' works well, or simply recognise where the thought comes from – for instance, 'This is just a lie my father/teacher/friend told me.'

3. Concentrate on success

If you have low self-esteem you'll tend to forget your achievements or play them down. Make a list of your successes, however trivial they may seem – from learning to ride a bike or swimming a width to having a baby or getting a new job. Now try this powerful technique from NLP (Neuro-Linguistic Programming – a therapy that gives you neurological strategies for improving performance) :

1. Remember exactly how you felt when you experienced your biggest achievement. For example, the day you passed your driving test; when you got the letter saying you'd got the job; when they put your baby in your arms?

2. Play the scene over and over, making it as real as possible. Recall how you felt inside yourself, what you heard (both from outside and inside your head), what you saw, what you felt physically, maybe what you smelt or tasted.

3. Each time you feel fully suffused by the emotions and experiences of the scene, 'anchor' that feeling by squeezing your hand into a fist.

4. Repeat this at least ten times, one after the other.

Eventually you will find that simply by making the fist you will be able to recreate the feeling on demand and, whenever you start to feel hopeless or useless, you can make a fist and bring back that feeling of achievement. I use this whenever I have a tough situation to face and might be feeling a bit low in the confidence stakes – a prime example is when I have to go on a live television show or speak to a crowd of people.

Banishing limiting beliefs

Sometimes you will do all this work and still find you are left with a series of limiting belief patterns. You might find yourself saying, 'I can't do that because' or, 'Yes, but it wouldn't work for *me* because'. You're not being the awkward squad: it's purely because psychologically we rebel against changing beliefs that have been embedded in our psyches (I'm not good enough, I can't say no to my boss, I can never have a loving relationship, and so on). Our psyches abhor change. If you encounter a lot of resistance to these exercises, it may be that your psyche is feeling unsteady and so clings on to the old self-image, however damaging or negative. If so, you won't get far by forcing it to change. Instead, you need to adopt a more playful, less pressurised approach. Try asking yourself:

- Which belief would I *rather* hold around this issue?
- If I were someone who believed this, how would I know? What would I do that would be different?
- If I believed this, which actions would I take? Make a list. For example: 'If I believed that already, I would spend far less this week/walk to the gym every morning/get up early and meditate.'
- How *precisely* might you make those changes? Think of action steps you could take.
- Now try them in your life.

'It is easy and light,' says Lisa Wynn who often uses this technique:

You are not asking someone to believe that they are capable even of being this new person. Instead you are showing curiosity and just making the space for them to start being the person with the new belief. Once you take an action step (one that is do-able), you start to build up evidence that the new belief is true. Once that truth is accepted, the old belief has to dissolve because there is no room for it in the new psyche.

Another variation of this is a sort of self-help parlour game called Playing Oprah. I first did this in a weekend retreat with spiritual fitness coach Caroline Reynolds and found it a brilliant way of psyching myself up for change. It is also hilariously good fun.

Playing Oprah

You'll need one or two good friends to help you with this. You also all need to be willing to let go of your inhibitions. This is a game – it's supposed to be fun.

Basically you pretend that you are the guest on a chat show. *Oprah* is a good one, but you could be on *Richard & Judy* or whatever you fancy. Your friend(s) is/are the chat-show host(s). You have come on the show to talk about your incredible success in beating your own personal overload and achieving your new blissful life.

You know what happens on these shows. The host starts by giving you the most incredible ego-boost, telling the audience how successful you have been. He or she then turns to you and asks how you did it. How *precisely* did you get from that awful place to this wonderful one? What were your strategies? What tips could you pass on to this eager audience? How do you feel now you have your perfect life? It's not threatening to the subconscious, because it's a game. Yet it's a very clever game because all the time your subconscious is coming up with strategies that could actually work. By allowing your subconscious to find the way (rather than imposing edicts from the conscious mind) you stand much more chance of succeeding. And you may well be surprised at just how clever the suggestions are that come up.

Go on, try it. Go over the top. Be as inflated and boastful as you like. Can't do it? What would you be like if you *were* brimming with confidence? Pretend. Fake it.

The true Self

By boosting self-esteem, we can start to loosen up, to spot the traps that ego lays for us – and become more self-aware. Start to monitor your thoughts and feelings – and begin to recognise that they are merely thoughts and feelings; they are not the essential 'you'. Often we forget that emotions are just emotions – we say that we 'are angry' when really we are just experiencing the emotion of anger. Recognise, too, that our emotions are often revved up by our thoughts. You start thinking angry thoughts, which then turn into feelings of anger. It happens so quickly we're usually unaware of what's happening. Start by trying to notice your responses. What were the thoughts that made you angry? Is anger really the appropriate response? Possibly so but you could equally be just running an old pattern. Above all, realise that you always have a choice. The glass can be half-empty or half-full. You can identify with your fears, your emotions, your negative thoughts – or you can choose to rise above them.

You, and only you, are responsible for your inner space, how you feel and think inside.

Our true Self

Beyond the ego, the persona and all the quirks of our psyches, lies the Self: our essential essence. Our soul-centre. Our Self doesn't give a fig for the latest gadgets and fashions; status is irrelevant. The Self is the part of us that is eternal, it's the part that craves meaning, that needs a more spiritual purpose. When your Self starts crying out for meaning in your life, you simply *have* to lose overload and heed its call. Otherwise you will end up feeling soul-sick, weary to the very depths of your spirit. The great sadness nowadays is that we have lost the habit of soul work. We expect to find our souls in an hour-long session or by buying into designer spirituality. No. Soul work is slow and often tough. Over the next few chapters we'll look at ways of heeding your Self's needs.

Chapter 14

Now: the key to happiness

Our society is dogged by the twin plagues of depression and anxiety. If we are overloaded, we usually suffer from one, if not both. When you look more deeply at these afflictions, they are (for the most part) caused by over-identification with either the past or the future. We become anxious about things that might happen, or might not happen, or might happen in the wrong way. Anxiety (and its cohorts: tension, worry, stress and fear) is always looking ahead, it is always worried about the future. It can base its concerns on the past – how things went wrong before (and so might well do again), but primarily it is a fear of the future. Depression, however, often comes about from things that went awry in the past and a belief that things won't become right ever again in the future. Depression is often founded on malaises of the past – regret, resentment, grief, bitterness and grudge-holding.

When we are overloaded we frequently become paralysed by anxiety. If we move towards burnout, we often allow ourselves to drop into the slough of depression; we simply cut off. The answer to both (and to beating overload into the ground) is living in the Now, the present, this moment and then the next and then the next. It's very Zen, and totally life-transforming. This isn't just New Age mumbo-jumbo – it's science fact. Our emotions affect our thoughts. Our posture affects our emotions. There are clear biochemical links between our feelings, our thoughts and our physiological responses. Emotions literally turn into neuropeptides (biochemicals) in the brain and lock into receptor sites in our cells – these chemical changes affect our actions. Dr Candace Pert, the US pharmacologist and mind–body expert says, 'We know we can drastically shift our moods and emotions with psycho-active drugs, but we also know now that we can trigger these states with different emotional states, too. Emotions are the link between the physical and the mental realms.' So, yes, thoughts can harm, thoughts can heal. Even a small shift of focus could change your entire life.

A word on depression and anxiety

Some people develop depression out of purely physiological reasons. I always advise anyone suffering from depression to visit his or her physician and ask for a thorough check-up. Your brain chemicals could be out of sync or you could have hormonal imbalances. Problems with the thyroid gland, in particular, frequently cause depression. Other medical causes include glandular fever, anaemia, adrenal problems and diabetes. Food allergies and candida can create mood imbalances; so, too, can vitamin and mineral deficiencies. If you're taking any medication, interactions between various drugs can be a common factor.

If there is no physiological problem, I would suggest you ask for counselling or psychotherapy. This has been shown to be as effective as medication for low- to mid-line depression. Severe depression may require medication.

If anxiety is ruining your life, I would also advise you to find help. Psychotherapy, hypnotherapy, NLP and EMDR (eye movement desensitisation reprogramming) can all be enormously helpful. Don't suffer in silence – there is no shame in either depression or anxiety, they are simply by-products of our overloaded society.

Herbal supplements can help, too. St John's Wort (*hypericum*) has been proven to be as effective as anti-depressants for moderate depression. However, check with your doctor before taking it if you are on any medication, as it can interact with several drugs, including the birth-control pill. *Rhodiola rosea* is another 'good mood' herb that I have found very useful in helping people suffering from both depression and anxiety. There are no known side effects, but do not take if you are pregnant or breast-feeding.

Living in the Now

Jo Pickering, founder of The Retreat Company, says succinctly, 'If we can move away from this collective belief in not enough time, I feel we would begin to reverse the overload treadmill. We can move away from chaos and confusion by spending time just being in the Now.' Wise words. Virtually everyone I spoke to during the research for this book said the same thing: practise living in the Now (not the 'then' and not the 'yet to come').

Why do we constantly dwell in the past or project into the future? Once again, you can blame a poorly developed ego. It's your anxious ego that pokes its nose into the future and goads you into anxiety, saying, 'You'll only be OK when you've got this, or achieved that.' It's a weak ego that holds on to past grudges, disappointments and failures and can't say, 'Enough! Time to move on.' In fact, when you think about it, there really is no past or future, there is only now. The present moment is all we have, it's the part of our life in which we live. The past is gone, for good or ill. The future will be what it will be. So how come most of us insist on living in the past or the future? Of course, it's fine to visit the past from time to time. It's good to remind yourself of happy memories, of good times, of strategies that worked for you and those that didn't. Of course you should have plans, goals and hopeful anticipation for the future. Without those, you would be unlikely to move on in life. However, try to move towards living in the present for more of your life and you will certainly relieve overload.

Dr Pert says, 'The minute the chemicals meet the receptor sites, they send signals that tell us to think and behave as we did before, *unless we break the cycle.* As adults we are operating as if today was yesterday. All our responses are a pattern.' Note my italics – it *is* possible to break the cycle. We can take responsibility and change.

The wonder of Now

When you begin to be aware of each moment, when you live your life in the Now, you start to notice the sheer wonder of life. It's a huge boon for overloaded lives. Say you had only ten minutes to play with your child. In the normal stressed response you would be worrying about how little time you had, thinking ahead to what you had to do afterwards. You might feel guilty about not spending enough time with your child, maybe even resentful of your child that she or he were taking up your time. When you live in the Now that transforms entirely. You simply make the most of each moment, engaging fully with your child. You might not build a whole brick house or complete a puzzle or a story, but you will have *been* with that child, 100 per cent for those ten minutes. When your time is up, you may feel sad that you couldn't continue but you know that you have had ten magic minutes.

Now provides magic throughout any day. Even mundane tasks become interesting when you live in every second, when every moment becomes a meditation. Even everyday tasks like doing the washing, or walking to work, become new and fresh when you take them one moment at a time.

If you don't feel you have enough right now, when will you have enough?

We postpone our happiness, we put our lives on hold, we allow ourselves to become overloaded and stressed, because we constantly project into the future. When your life is somewhere in the future, how can you enjoy your 'real' life, here and now? We all do it – you're not alone. We all think we'll be happy when we get the new job, when we move to that great house, when we lose weight, when we have a healthy bank balance. Happiness is elusive – grab it while you can. Start looking around your life and noticing the small things – the hair on the back of your child's neck, the tiny perfection of a daisy, the pattern of a cloud. Yes, it sounds corny, but so what? Relax into the lovely moments, your partner's hug, a comfortable chair, a great meal. Notice the workings of your body – stretch your muscles, listen to your heartbeat, breathe deeply. Think about what happiness really is. It's not some miraculous God-given state of being – it's simply a series of great moments one after another. Tack enough together and you end up with a free-fall run of happiness.

Are you avoiding happiness?

So many of us scupper our happiness by avoiding the present, probably because living in the Now can be pretty confrontational. Meditation teachers usually warn that when you come into the moment, old fears, emotions, revelations and realities can surface. Workaholics in particular also tend to shy away from intimacy, true connection with other people. It's often easier to criticise our partner or fantasise about a new, perfect lover, than to try to reach real connection, true intimacy. It's simpler to get huffy and irritated about the person we're forced to sit next to on a bus or plane, than it is to smile and perhaps engage in conversation. It's easier to be cynical and mocking, rather than allow ourselves to be open and vulnerable.

Once again, give yourself the time to think about what you really want from life. Recap the work we did on beliefs and values in the last chapter. In addition, ask yourself:

1. Am I happy? What would make me happy?
2. What do I need to do in my life to be free?
3. What parts of myself, both in the past and the present, have I hidden from others for fear they would disapprove of me? What parts do I bury even from myself?
4. What are *my* values and beliefs? If I lived them 100 per cent, how would that look in my life? How would the people close to me react?
5. Am I living where and how I want to live or where and how someone else wants me to live? What would I have to change to make my lifestyle congruous with my desires?

Concentrate on your feelings. Recognise that your needs change – what was good for you last year, or last week, may not work for you now.

Right now

Try the 'right now' mindfulness meditation.

1. Whatever you are doing, whether it is writing a report or sitting on a bus, or cooking dinner, concentrate on what you are actually doing.
2. Say to yourself, 'Right now I am sitting on the bus ... Right now I am listening to children laughing, the engine of the bus ... Right now I am breathing deeply ... Right now I am stretching.'

> **3.** Take deep, relaxing breaths between each 'right now'. Keep going for about five minutes and practise as often as you can.
>
> Review the meditation and breathing exercises in Chapter 11: The four super stress-reducers. Practise them regularly. Breathing, meditation and mindfulness are supreme ways of getting into the Now.

Start keeping a journal or diary – not of events particularly, but of your feelings, your observations, anything you noticed when you were in the Now. You don't have to write every day but make sure you are honest and record your thoughts without censorship. Look on it as practice for being happy – the more you recognise moments of joy, the more easily they will start to come the next time.

Sarah Dening suggests you give yourself time at the end of each day to reflect on the day that passed. Look at everything you did and ask yourself if you were pleased with your behaviour, your decisions. If so, give yourself a pat on the back. If not, ask yourself what you could have done differently and think that maybe you'll try that next time. It's not about blame – usually you find you made far more good decisions than bad.

Change your attitude

Remember that even if you can't change a situation you *can* change your attitude. If the present moment is not how you'd like it to be, don't rail against it. Accept it. If you can't shed it (that is, walk away) or shift it (change it), then you need to accept it. It's a vital lesson. Ask yourself how you could make it better. Remember: you are only looking at each moment – not the whole task or day.

> ### *This moment*
> How could *this* very moment be better?
> 1. Start with a breath.
> 2. Ask yourself if you have a problem, right now? Not a problem that might surface in a day or so, or an hour or so, or even five minutes' time. But right now? Everyone has problems – life always throws challenges our way. But bring it all back to the moment – what's your problem at this precise moment? Try it; it's an interesting exercise.

It's not just an exercise for work either – practise it at home, with your children (it's really useful for helping exam stress) or your partner. If you have committed to a person, then don't spend your entire life trying to change them. Remember, another great truth in life is that we can never change other people: we can only change ourselves and our own responses. Choose to be where you are every minute, accept that and give your whole being to the person and the moment. Look for the good bits rather than pouncing on the bad.

How else can you get into the Now? Stress expert Robert Holden recommends you start every day with what he calls the 'Newness of Life' game. He suggests you see each day as a newborn child would see the day: as a new day that has never happened before. Ask yourself, 'What can I look for, listen for, think about and do that is new today?' I love that idea. Going on from that, I'd suggest you try to spend time with children. Seeing the world through children's eyes can remind us how amazing, fascinating, interesting and 'wonder-full' so many things that surround us are, which we have come to take for granted. Don't let cynicism take you over. Keep your innocence and wonderment. Take a fresh look, be inquisitive. Smile. Laugh.

Accentuate the positive

When you are overloaded, it's easy to fall into negative thinking. It's natural to look at worst-case scenarios, to believe that if shit is going to happen, it's going to happen to you. As we've seen this can be a useful exercise when it allows you to put things in perspective. However, if you indulge in permanent negative thinking and worst-case scenarios, you can end up attracting them to you. Most people spend their lives thinking about what they *don't* want, about what might go wrong in their lives, and if those are the kinds of thoughts that go round in our minds, our subconscious will strive to bring them into manifestation in our lives.

The subconscious mind always tries to do what it's told. Tell it you're stressed and overloaded and it will seek to make that scenario real. It will advise your heart to pump faster, your skin to sweat, your mind to go into a tailspin of anxiety. It will seek out mess and confusion and propel you towards people who will panic and overload you even further. I'm not saying that all overload is imaginary – but we do contribute to our overload by bombarding our brains with the message that we can't cope.

Equally we can stifle our lives in the here and now by listening to old messages, to the sayings and beliefs that we heard as we grew up. Remember what we looked at earlier? Many people will never allow themselves to become rich or even comfortably well-off because they have subconsciously taken on board negative ideas about money from early life ('you have to slave for every penny'; 'money doesn't grow on trees'; 'don't be greedy', and so on).

Everyone fails sometimes – it's just part of life. But when you learn to live in the moment, you take it in your stride. Equally, you no longer put the onus for your happiness onto other people – you accept that it's your choice and your responsibility. We become so fixed on goals (money, power, possessions) that we forget to enjoy the journey of life. Don't spend your entire life waiting to start living.

Happiness or overload? Basically there's a choice. Look at the world with jaundiced, jaded, cynical eyes and it will overload you and irritate the hell out of you. You will always be yearning for a future life of impossible perfection. However, shift your perspective and see the beauty in small things, the joy in other people and the world will suddenly seem a brighter place.

Chapter 15

Authenticity

Work – whether it's managing a company or running a family – is usually the primary cause of overload. Interestingly, as we've already seen, it's not necessarily the most difficult, dangerous or demanding careers that cause the most stress and overload. When you're doing the job you love (providing it doesn't overburden your time and leave space for nothing else) you are far less likely to feel overloaded and overstretched. Boring, apparently pointless jobs are often far more exhausting than big, challenging, exciting jobs.

So why do so many of us endure, day after day, year after year, jobs we hate? Often we feel we have no choice. Maybe you spent a long time training for this job; maybe you have fallen in thrall to the salary or security or status the job entails. Maybe you have been brought up with the mindset that 'you can't be paid for work you enjoy' or 'you don't deserve to have fun at work'. Many of us are still stuck firmly in the protestant work ethic (I battle with it myself all the time). Maybe you feel you'd lose status if you shifted your career, or dumped your career. Maybe you feel it's too late to change or that change is scary. Well, yes it can be. But so, too, is spending the vast majority of your life doing work you hate and pushing yourself into overload in the process.

While researching this book I found much to be depressed about. The statistics on overload and stress were shocking. I felt almost despondent that society would not be willing to change. However, there were two movements that offered huge hope. One was the Slow Movement that we'll look at in the next chapter. The other was the fledgling Authentic Movement.

What is Authentic?

The Authentic Movement is a loose-knit independent alliance of like-minded people and companies in the UK who work with principles and passion. It encompasses all kinds of business – from manufacturers to marketing, from fashion to finance. The guiding principle is that primarily you do work that is true to your Self. However, many individuals and companies extend this so that their work has integrity towards the wider community and, in the broadest sense, the planet. It's ethical, but not remotely worthy and grim.

Many of the people I interviewed in the research for this book are active members of the Authentic Movement. Others, while not officially affiliated, have similar aims and beliefs. The work of authors like Nick Williams (*The Work We Were Born to Do*), Ben Renshaw (*Successful but Something Missing*), Lynn Franks (*The Seed Handbook*) and Rick Jarow (*Creating the Work You Love*) are also very much on this wavelength. I found their thoughts and optimism incredibly cheering, their advice extraordinarily wise. I'm going to start this chapter with some of their thoughts on how being authentic is part of the overload solution.

Neil Crofts, the founder of Authentic Business says:

The solution is for each and every one of us to make a decision and a promise to ourselves. The promise is that we will never again work without meaning, that we will never again sell our soul for a few trinkets and baubles. That we will not compromise our identity for the false promise of security. That we commit ourselves unconditionally to our own true happiness and purpose.

Astrologer and life coach Michael Geary says, 'Whatever you do, do something that you enjoy doing. Doing what you like gives you stamina, staying power, vision and patience. If you're in a dead end job, change it. Re-educate yourself if necessary. Consider your natural strengths and if possible find a job that uses them.'

Richard Jacobs, author of *What's Your Purpose?* says:

For me the solution is in finding and living our Purpose. Our Purpose is always greater than ourselves. Our Purpose is our greatest values, our gifts, talents and abilities combined with the contribution we would most like to make to the world. When we live our purpose, we become more intelligent, we lose our boundaries, generate inspiration in ourselves and others and live an adventure beyond the imaginings of even childhood fantasy.

Corporate consultant and healer Jonathan Chuter points out that being authentic does not have to equate with being poor:

We can be millionaires, but millionaires with heart – the two aren't mutually exclusive. It just means us dropping our old 'I'm better/richer than you are' programming and taking a fresh look at how we should lead our lives, and the values and attitudes behind how we earn our money. If we set out to 'screw' people financially, then we get screwed. It all comes back to us, as sure as eggs is eggs. Whatever we put out, we get back. By changing ourselves, we can change anything.

Notice he doesn't try to change other people or the world

directly. He says you have to change yourself first – totally key.

Lisa Wynn says she often asks clients three vital questions:

1. What do you want for the world?
2. What would you wave a magic wand over if you had a single wish for the world?
3. How can you incorporate your passion into your work?

She insists that, while we might not think it, many of us are fired by working for the greater good. How do *you* contribute to making the world a better place? What are you *The One* for? What do you bring to the world, and what do you want to create? 'Having asked hundreds of people what they want from work, I hear most often that people want to contribute, to be heard and to express their gifts and potential,' says Lisa.

It's not necessarily about being a volunteer for charity or doing 'good works' – but about making a difference, in some small way, on a regular basis. A hairdresser makes people feel better about themselves, a box office attendant facilitates people being able to enjoy the arts, a cleaner makes the environment better for people – you get the picture?

Sarah Dening sums it up beautifully:

> When you are authentic, when you are being truly real, in harmony with yourself, you are simply not going to feel over-loaded. So you might say there is a correlation between overload and being *inauthentic*. Maybe you have a need for approval, a need to please people, or a martyr complex, or you need to have a certain status. Yet in your inmost *you*, your authentic you, that really doesn't matter so much.

How to be authentic

You can be authentic or inauthentic in all parts of your life. Look back at your list of values. Are you being true to them in all areas of your life? If not, how could you change? Often work is the hardest part, so let's look at that in more detail. First of all, acknowledge that you have been working very hard, doing your best but that now it could be time for a change. Give yourself enough time to look long and hard at your work and your career options. Many of us made our decisions about our life work when we were still at school, when we were children or adolescents. What sounded good then might not be so hot now. Remember, also, that we change. As we move through life we develop and deepen – the media career that was so exciting when you were a teenager can pall into meaningless boredom when you hit 30.

Give yourself plenty of time to work with these exercises. Few of us take the time to analyse precisely why we do the work we do and where exactly the problems lie. Although you may insist 'I hate my job', it is worth sitting down and asking *exactly* what it is you hate about it. It might well be only one element of your work that you dislike. Remember this applies just as much to those people who don't think they 'work' as such – full-time carers, parents, homekeepers. Frankly, looking after children, the elderly or people with disabilities is about the toughest job you can get.

As you do these exercises, put down everything you can think of, however silly or unrelated it may appear. Some people have made incredible careers by unearthing skills and pleasures from things they did at school or at the youth club. Others have founded wonderful businesses by turning a hobby into a job.

1. Look at your family script

We learn many of our deep-seated beliefs about work at a very young age from previous generations for whom the concept of work was often intrinsically bound up with notions of duty, of discipline, of hard slog. Consequently, we end up following other people's work scripts, obeying decisions we made *almost subconsciously* about work before we even entered the workplace.

1. What are your core beliefs about work? For example, do you think 'I always get to be the deputy, never the boss'; 'I have to have a "proper" professional career, like a doctor or lawyer'? 'I could never run my own business'; 'A woman's place is in the home'?

2. From where did those thoughts come? Did you feel unsatisfied at school? Was your father never promoted beyond a certain level? Did your parents tell you how much your education was costing and that you owed it to them to get a sensible job? Were you told it was 'your duty' to stay at home?

3. Decide whether these are appropriate thoughts now. If not, be willing to let them go. Merely by being aware of your internal script you can re-assess your pattern.

2. Find your job personality

You can now look at what you really want from your work, what will support *you*. Make an audit of all your skills, your knowledge, your attributes and qualities, your hobbies. Start as early as you like and put down *everything* you can think of: subjects you learnt at school and college; jobs and the skills and qualities they called for; extra-curricular activities and hobbies you enjoyed; workshops or trainings.

1. Are there any patterns, any subjects you have always enjoyed; any skills that you have used throughout your life and which you enjoy? Which are your favourite three skills and your favourite three areas of knowledge? Exactly how do you like using your skills?

2. You may well feel you would like to develop a skill or start using an old skill again. You might consider that your

present job really doesn't represent your true skills and breadth of knowledge. Jot down any thoughts that come into your head and then move on.

3. The ideal workplace

On the other hand, your present job might use all your skills and knowledge. The problem could well be *where* you are working. Question the context in which you want to use your skills.

1. In what kind of organisation would you be happiest? Large, small, your own? Public or private sector? What would it do (make things, disseminate information, help people, and so on)? Would the workforce be primarily male, female, or mixed? Would you work alone, in a small team, as part of a large structure?
2. Could you change your work environment? For instance, instead of teaching large groups of adults, could you give one-to-one help to children with special needs?
3. If you are lonely working on your own, perhaps you could become part of a team or under the auspices of a larger department that would give support and feedback.

4. Your work language

What kind of language do you listen to all day long in your workplace? Do you spend your days talking in accountant-speak, or library-lingo, or teacher-talk? More to the point, do you enjoy the language of your workplace? Lots of people have discovered that they enjoy the skills they use but hate the language they have to speak. But a solicitor does not have to speak just solicitese; she could also speak the language of film or theatre; of medicine; of psychology; of shipping, depending on the area of law in which she

chooses to pursue her skills. An administrator might love
his job, might feel very happy with the size and structure of
the organisation for which he works but simply hate the
fact that it deals in military uniforms because, over the last
few years, his views on defence have fundamentally
changed.

5. Creating your ideal job

Now you should have most of the information you require
to discover your ideal work situation. Pull it all together
and find the anatomy of your ideal job.

1. Ask yourself what your dreams are – if this were the last day
   of your life what would you regret not ever having done?
   Incorporate any answers into your job anatomy. Indulge in
   some playful thinking around matching your favourite
   pursuits to possible jobs. Be inventive, be silly, don't
   analyse. Try to think of ways to link even the most incon-
   gruous qualities; use it as a test of your lateral thinking.

2. Now go out and get your job. Don't wait for an advertise-
   ment. Find a company that fits your needs and approach
   them. Truly, I know many people who have had jobs literally created for them after offering their services to their
   ideal employer. For example, Sandra successfully persuaded a large corporation to set up an in-house crèche, with
   her in charge. John persuaded a local estate agent that
   they were missing a trick, not having an overseas property
   department – they agreed, and hired him. Rachel, an
   accountant, loved her job and company but hated the
   commute: she suggested a home-working package and
   now goes into the office twice a month.

3. Or start your own business. Why not? Suzy wanted to spend
   more time at home with her young children, so she ditched
   her IT sales job and set up a website selling lingerie. Nicky

> worked for years as a marketing manager but realised she loved networking and set up her own recruitment agency. In his fifties, Peter hated his job in advertising but knew he'd find it tough to get another job at his age so he launched into web design and has never looked back.

Refining the search: the Core Statement

I love this process. While the exercises above are all very rational and logical, the Core Statement recognises that being authentic is also an exercise in imagination, in creativity, in jumping out of the box. I learnt about the Core Statement many years ago from psychotherapist Sheila MacLeod, and have used it repeatedly since then. The aim, says Sheila, is to discover what would make you truly happy, to discover the kind of role in life that could make your 'soul sing.'

It's about more than work: the Core Statement is a clear and concise statement of your life's purpose. It outlines the criteria that have to be fulfilled in order to keep you contented and committed to your path in life – to make you adore your days rather than suffer overload and boredom. We all have quite specific roles we feel happiest playing in life. Whereas one person might adore new challenges, another might love nothing better than the safe and secure.

Our Core Statement tends to be clearest in childhood, before we succumbed to the pressures of school and work. Unfortunately, many of us veer away from that straight path – either from pressure at school or college or in the workplace. Sheila says:

'The language is always poetic, almost mystical, but it has to resonate within you. For some people the core might be very quiet, for example, "I ensure everything is in its place." It's like being given the master key to your life.'

Finding your Core Statement

Start to understand what makes you 'sing your song' by thinking about the following. It helps if you can work with another person who can pick up on the phrases you emphasise or repeat. If that isn't possible, record your responses and listen very carefully to what you say.

1. Find a joyful childhood memory. Have your partner ask you the following:
   - What were you doing?
   - What made it special for you?
   - How did you feel?
   - Was anyone with you?
   - Which aspect did you enjoy the most?

   Write down the key phrases and words that occur.

2. Think of a good time in your life – at any period. Ask the same questions as before and again write down any key phrases and words.

3. Repeat the above process with the following:
   - Talk about a fulfilling work experience
   - Explore a hobby or pastime
   - Capture a moment when you felt complete

4. Now find the most important phrases and words.
   - Which keep occurring?
   - Where are the patterns?
   - Which represent the most important circumstances or attitudes?

   If you could have only three or four of these phrases or words, which would they be?

5. Try to incorporate these phrases into a sentence that has real meaning for you.

Sheila MacLeod says that when you hit on the right kind of statement it will instinctively feel right – some people laugh or even cry. Play with it until it works for you. One sales executive was bored rigid with his job until he realised that he needed the thrill and challenge of a commission-only basis. His poetic statement was: 'Standing on the edge of the universe, I roar.' A news journalist realigned herself into in-depth investigations after uncovering her statement: 'Digging deep for secrets, patient power, silent and slow.'

For the majority of us, work occupies the largest part of our waking life. Don't live for Fridays and spend Sunday dreading Monday. Don't count the days until retirement. Don't endure a job you hate. You *can* change your job to reflect your interests, your beliefs, your strengths and your personality. Become authentic in your work and love the way you spend your days.

Chapter 16

Downshift, simplify and slow down

Should you downshift? According to research from Cambridge University, that's exactly what around a quarter of people between the ages of 30 and 59 have done, as they voluntarily made a long-term change in their lives that resulted in them earning, on average, 40 per cent less. The most common reason given for the phenomenon was to 'spend more time with their family' and to 'recapture control over their time'. Sounds familiar? The three principal methods of downshifting are reducing working hours, stopping work altogether or changing careers. The most common way people in the study funded this was to sell their property and move to a smaller place or to a cheaper location.

Of course, this works only if you are lucky enough to own a house with enough equity for you to sell and buy a cheaper one without a mortgage or with a much-reduced mortgage. If you're in that position, it's a very alluring proposition. However, do your sums. Remember that house buying and selling is costly – some people find that, by the time they have factored in lawyers' and agents' fees plus the hugely hiked stamp duty and tax, moving costs and any redecoration needed, they aren't any better off.

Look long and hard at what you really want from life; be realistic.

> ***Paul***, a civil servant, and Eva, a PA, threw in their jobs, sold their city house and moved to the countryside. Within a year, they were bored rigid and desperate to return both to work and to city life.

There is actually a recognised *under*load syndrome – with many of the same symptoms of overload. Boredom can be stressful, too.

If you relocated, where would you relocate? Would you have to spend more to live there (in travel costs, schooling, and so on)? Do your homework very thoroughly. The countryside can appear very attractive but there *are* downsides. For instance, we bought a big house for the price of a small flat in the city, but we have to run two cars because we're so isolated (and one of them needs to be a 4×4 to get out when it snows). It's a 40-minute trip to the nearest supermarket and we're an hour away from our nearest department store. Going to the cinema becomes a major excursion and we never have takeaways because the meal is stone cold and congealed by the time it arrives (oh, and we have to go and get it, nobody delivers this far out). The land and outbuildings we thought so enchanting, take time, money and hard work to maintain. Our heating bills are higher, because we don't have the warm insulation of other houses around us. However, we balance this against the clean air, lack of crime, and stunning views (and we don't spend so much, because temptation is at arm's length), but it's not to everyone's taste.

Many people who move here find the isolation, lack of facilities and dearth of like-minded people just too much, and rush back to the city. The same story happens all over the country and also abroad. What seems great while you're on holiday can pall when you're there all year round. How do the locals react to incomers? Would you be welcomed if you didn't speak the language? Could you work? What is the local education like? What would you miss from your old life? Do your homework very thoroughly. Ask people who are already living there for the downsides as well as the upsides.

Remember, too, that once you downshift it can be tough to get back to where you once were (should you wish to). Paul and Eva had to settle for a much smaller apartment when they returned to London because house prices in the capital had risen far more swiftly than in the country. Also, for many people, pensions are a lost cause and their home *is* their pension. It all needs careful thought. Having said that, it's still well worth considering.

Downshifting your home can take a huge pressure from your life. Just imagine what having fewer or no debts could mean to you. It might offer the possibility of wonderful holidays. Or more time together as a family or a couple. It might provide the means for you to look at different career options, at starting up your own business, or pursuing more creative goals.

Chris (a graphic designer) and Helen (a chef) hated their jobs and the status envy pervasive in their South-east town so they sold up and bought a small farm in Devon. Chris took evening classes in plumbing to bring in essential cash while Helen devoted herself to the B&B business and their 'good life' smallholding. They no longer drive smart cars or have luxurious holidays but don't give a toss. They say that 'every day is like a holiday. We're living our dream.'

Bear in mind that downshifting doesn't necessarily have to

mean a huge move, and it doesn't have to involve the country-side either. If you enjoy the buzz, the culture and sociability of city life, you could move to a cheaper city, or to a cheaper neighbourhood, or to the suburbs. In fact, the downshifting trend is not, in fact, as fantasy-driven as the TV shows would have us believe; whereas many people *are* heading for the countryside or overseas, the majority are shunting down the line to suburbia. Do you need the size house you have? I know many people who have divested themselves of their large hous-es and felt the freedom of being debt-free in smaller houses or apartments. You have to keep asking yourself what is most important to *your* life.

It's not just houses

Finding the means to downshift isn't just about houses either. Do you need such a big car – or any car at all if you live in an urban area? It can be much cheaper (and less hassle) to hire a car for the odd trip out of town. Is your child in private educa-tion because it's the only choice? A hot-house education can be a misery for modern children. Pick schools, activities and tutor-ing to suit your child, not *your* expectations and craving for status. Are fancy holidays really necessary? Maybe you could have as much fun on a cheap seaside holiday as on a luxurious exclusive cruise. Once again, ask the Miracle Question about all these options. For example, how would you know you were on your ideal holiday? How would your family know? A holiday is about time out with the people you like or love the most (or on your own for peace and quiet). Check out early bird and last-minute deals. Think laterally – go to unusual destinations or stay close to home.

Christmas and birthdays can be hugely expensive. Once again, they can be downsized without losing any of the magic or fun. We kid ourselves that things have to be perfect (remember perfection is one of the demons of overload) and lose sight of the real importance of such festivals. They should come down to people, not things. As the economist E F Schumacher, author of *Small is Beautiful*, said: 'Money is not the measure of all things – we live in a society not an economy.'

Above all, remember that money is rarely the means to happiness. Research shows that the most important factor in providing happiness is good close social relationships. The happiest people are those who have good marriages, good friends, and who are close to their families. Interestingly, having a religion, a faith or a sense of spirituality is another happiness factor.

That's well worth remembering when you make your choices. And you *do* have a choice. 'The solution to overload is to "choose"', says Brian Mayne, co-author of *Life Mapping*. 'Make a fundamental *choice* about the pace you want to live, the quality of life you want to enjoy, and then make your plans to move towards it.'

Many people find that, by having lower and cheaper expectations, they can afford to drop their hours, or shift from a high-paying job they hate to a lower-paying one that gives them huge satisfaction. Others take the plunge into starting new businesses or retraining.

Simplify

Whether or not you are in a position to downshift, you can still ease overload by simplifying your life. In many ways simplification is just as key as downshifting. As we saw in the first part of *The Overload Solution*, our psyches don't like anything incomplete or unfinished. If we're juggling too many balls, our brain consistently thinks about each and every one of them. The complexity of our modern overloaded lives becomes draining.

Simplicity is the solution to complexity. Less choice is the solution to overwhelming choice. A simple life is usually a cheaper life. If you were to live simply you might not necessarily need that all-encompassing, all-demanding job. You could get by with shorter hours, part-time working, or simply doing work as and when you need it. A friend of mine sussed the corporate rat race a long time ago and gave up her high-profile job in marketing and her big expensive house. Instead she rents a small apartment and works as and when she needs to for a local call-centre (she's an expert communicator so it doesn't cause her the stress it might for other people). The time she has freed up she uses to travel, to write screenplays and to indulge her passion for amateur dramatics. She laughs out loud at the idea of working to satisfy ego and gives the finger to corporate life.

Ask yourself:

How have I overloaded my life with people and things?

We're told it's good to have a second home; that we should aspire to having expensive cars (note the plural), fancy sports equipment, state-of-the-art technology, a massive wardrobe. We're encouraged to collect things. Some of us yearn for motorbikes, boats, horses – you name it, we want it. But all these things take incredible upkeep. The fancier the equipment, the more attention it needs. Basic cars rarely go wrong – highly sophisticated cars that require computerised tune-ups are far more temperamental. A good old mongrel dog is tough as old boots, while her thoroughbred (*over*bred) cousin will have you down the vet every other week. Complicated things make for complicated lives.

If you want to simplify your life, take a look at this list. I'm not suggesting you follow all of it (we're all different and what causes me overload might be a breeze for you).

- Get rid of all the stuff that you don't use. Be brutal. Are you hoarding equipment for sports or hobbies you never use? Are you clinging on to old clothes in the hopes they will fit again – treat yourself to new ones if you lose those pounds. Do you keep stuff out of sentimentality? Let go of the past and enjoy the present.

- Question your collections. Do you really love them or are they just a way of telling people who you are? Maybe you have outgrown them. Your new healthy ego doesn't need external proof of who you are.
- Use things that you can fix yourself as far as possible.
- Cancel or cut down on your memberships of societies and clubs. Only keep those you really enjoy.
- Cancel or cut down on magazine and periodical subscriptions. They just urge you to buy more stuff.
- Cut out or cut down on Internet newsgroups, bulletin boards, chat rooms, favourite sites.
- Simplify shopping – use the same shops, choose the same brands that you know are good. Shop on-line for bulk-buy basics; support local shops for everyday needs.
- Make lists of nutritious meals for the week and create a shopping list for the week's needs. Some people find it liberating to use the same menus for a few weeks at a time. For example, if it's Monday it must be chowder.

The house and garden

Low-maintenance in the home equals more time to unwind:

- Make your garden/yard as low-maintenance as possible. Pave over small areas of lawn; fill borders with perennials; make the most of ground-cover plants.
- Get rid of houseplants – enjoy fresh flowers instead.
- Keep your house low-maintenance, too: clear all clutter; avoid fiddly ornaments; choose tough-wearing, easily maintained flooring, work surfaces and soft furnishings.
- If you want a pet keep it short haired (less likely to shed) and brindle (less likely to show if it does shed). White and long-haired is the overload nightmare, a prescription for major cleaning, specialist vacuums, grooming, hairballs. Don't go there.

- Buy second-hand cars that can be repaired at your local garage.
- Have potluck suppers or picnics for entertaining, or meet friends at local restaurants. If you want to go it alone, pick cook-ahead casseroles, curries or soups.
- Simplify gift giving – buy everyone the same thing. A book you adored, a CD you loved, a 'best-ever' toy. Pick one design of Christmas card – much, much simpler.
- Use the library. It needs your support and you won't clutter your life with one-time read books.
- Don't feel compelled to pick up the phone. Use voicemail, even at home and answer calls in your own time. Feel guilty? Turn down the volume.
- Do one thing at a time, mindfully. It's the polar opposite of multitasking and is much less stressful and much more efficient.

I remember a time when the house next door to my apartment went up in flames and it looked as if our building was going to follow. I had that classic moment of thinking, 'What do I take?' I snatched my handbag and my cat – and jumped to safety. As we sat, watching the flames, I truly felt it would not be the end of the world to lose everything and start again.

If you had to leave your house in an emergency, what could you not live without?

Whereas simplifying and decluttering come naturally to me, my husband is one of life's natural hoarders. So, what do you do if your partner doesn't want to simplify? Again, remember you can't change anyone, only yourself, so look at the parts of your own life you can simplify. Our compromise is that Adrian keeps his barrage of stuff in his office and up in the attic. It's not ideal but at least our communal areas are kept as clear as possible.

Remember that most stuff is about ego. It presents an image of who you think you should be to the world. But, as we've seen, your ego is not your true Self. The true Self needs very little. However, the true Self does need time, and that is our next focus.

Slowing down and stopping

When we are accustomed to living overloaded bloated lives, when we are used to following the dictates of a fragile ego, slowing down is scary, and stopping is downright terrifying. Our frantic busyness prevents us looking at the big questions. Many people find that, once they slow down or stop being overloaded, they have to reassess their relationships. I once watched a television programme in which two parents were racing around after their hyperactive, insomniac children. They complained that they never had time with one another. When the experts sorted out the children's problem, it left the parents with plenty of time – but nothing to say to one another. Their busyness had masked the fact that they had grown apart. Within a year they had separated.

Just consider the possibility of slowing down. Check out *In Praise of Slow*, a great book by the journalist Carl Honoré, who went in search of the burgeoning Slow Movement that is insinuating its way through Europe.

Honoré's wake-up moment came when he saw a book called *The One-Minute Bedtime Story* – classic fairy stories condensed into 'sixty-second sound bites'. He realised his whole life had become an 'exercise in hurry' so he went on an odyssey to discover the joys of slow and found it lead to better health, better work and business, better family life and relationships, better food and even better sex. 'Slow' is not about living at a snail's pace, it's not about turning Luddite or heading for the hills to live in log cabins; it's about balance. It's about spending enough time on the things that matter so that you can actually experience and enjoy them. The Slow Movement begs you to control the rhythms of your own life, to determine your own tempo.

Going slow *can* cut down overload without a shadow of a doubt – the very concept is incompatible with overload. Hence, I would say that it's usually tough to go slow in a major way until you have already downshifted or simplified your life. However, you *can* adopt some of the strategies into an over-loaded lifestyle and, in fact, slow can make you realise just how overloaded you are. For example, if you really don't have time to sit down and eat a meal, your life urgently needs re-assessing!

How do you go slow? Start looking beneath our linear, arrow-straight watch-time for other rhythms. In the past we would have noticed and celebrated the passing of the seasons. We would have marked the natural progress of the day – daylight segueing into twilight and on into dark. We would have noticed the cycles of the moon and its effects on our bodies and the natural world around us. We would have had one day a week that was holy, set aside for soul work. Now we ride roughshod over such transitions.

If that's a bit esoteric, here are some down-to-earth practical suggestions:

- Cram less in. Make wise choices. Stop multitasking.
- Create margins around your life. An hour off here, a day off there.
- Keep one day a week as a Sabbath – clear from mundane tasks, shopping, and so on. Use it for soul work – meditation, prayer, contemplation – and for your family.
- Have a cut-off point. Working all round the clock is not time-efficient – it interferes with sleep, butchers creativity and decreases productivity.
- Refuse to be hurried and harried by people. Breathe, smile and take your time.

Glorious food

- Slow food is real food – healthy food. In the time it takes you to heat up a microwave ready-meal you could have made a great salad, some warming soup, an omelette or real pasta sauce.
- Buy organic from local producers or subscribe to a weekly organic box.
- Boycott fast food. It's packed with potentially dangerous chemicals, makes you fat and encourages you to gorge your food, rather than savouring it.
- Eat at a table. Say some form of Grace. Concentrate on your food. Don't distract yourself with books or TV. Chew thoroughly – it will improve your digestion and prevent you piling on pounds.
- Eat together as a family. Children from families that regularly share meals are more likely to do well at school, less likely to smoke and drink at an early age, and are less prone to stress and overload.

- Allow holidays to be relaxing. Resist 'doing' holidays; stop notching up experiences. Think about how little you could do.
- Seek out things that are made with care and craftsmanship, rather than mass-produced synthetic trash.
- Garden – get your hands dirty. Or get out into nature on a regular basis. A tree wouldn't dream of throwing out new leaves in winter. A bulb wouldn't put off coming up in spring. It's only us humans who have lost all sight of the wisdom of doing things at the right and natural time, in the right and natural way.

Don't rush sex

When it comes to sex, slower is definitely better. Why settle for a quickie when you can enjoy a long, languorous hour or more of sheer pleasure? One of the best things I ever did was to study the Indian art of Tantra, sexual yoga.

According to Kinsey, the famous American sex researcher, 75 per cent of men ejaculate within two minutes of penetration. A Tantric lover can keep it going for as long as he chooses – slow heaven.

- Do your housework with care and mindfulness – make it a meditation. Choose natural products (salt, vinegar, baking powder, essential oils – not products that just put 'Natural' in their title but still contain chemicals).

- Relinquish the power of the clock. If you can, live part (or all) of your life without a watch. My husband never wears a watch and swears it makes him far less stressed (yet somehow he's never late). I confess I can't do this one.

- Drive within the speed limit. Driving too fast causes tension and strain. Bear in mind, too, that speed limits have a purpose. Hit a child at 40mph and she or he will most likely die; hit a child at 30mph and she or he will most likely live. Think about that as you speed through built-up areas or whiz through small country villages.

- Consult an alternative practitioner. The average GP spends six minutes with each patient. The average natural health practitioner spends an hour. Natural health is about preventative medicine, too. Your practitioner will look at ways of dealing with stress, he will adjust your diet, suggest exercises, possibly teach you meditation or relaxation.

- Take up art, or read poetry, or read books – but slowly. Try consciously to read slowly, taking in the sheer beauty of the prose.

Retreat – stopping in your tracks

Above all, have regular times for doing absolutely nothing. Start with five minutes and build up to an hour. Move on to a morning, graduate to a whole day or weekend. Don't plan anything at all.

Once more I urge you to go on retreat. Silent retreats are one of the greatest gifts you can give to your soul. One of the defining experiences of my life was a week-long silent retreat. At first it seemed strange, rude even, not to talk to people. I realised how much I was, at heart, a people pleaser, keen to ingratiate myself, and also how my ego was feeling insecure, unable to define myself through my work. After all, 'What do you do?' is the first thing we ask people nowadays. But after a day I relaxed into it and the liberation was enormous. Just being. No demands. No pressure. Divine. It cured me once and for all of the need for constant chitchat, to run the ego's stream of consciousness. I used to find silence awkward, now I relax into it. Try it yourself.

Chapter 17

Death – the teacher of life

We all die. It's the one certainty in life. Yet most of us steadfastly refuse to think about death. We shut it away from our consciousness and try to pretend it doesn't exist, that it won't happen if we don't think about it. Our attempts to shy away from death would be comical if they weren't so tragic. I once interviewed a group of 'immortalists' – people who firmly believed that they alone would never die. They were delightful people, full of vigour and verve – they were also in the prime of life. A few years later I bumped into one of them and inquired after one of his co-immortalists. 'Ah,' said the man, 'um, he died. Car accident.' It was sad but it was also blackly humorous. He shouldn't have died so soon but it was a delusion to imagine he could dodge death. A delusion based on fear.

Death is frightening for many reasons. Primarily it's unknown, the last great mystery. However, we also fear death because of our insecure egos – we hate the idea of losing our material possessions, our status, our loved ones, our sense of 'I'. As we've already discussed, most of us spend our lives surrounding ourselves with symbols of security and status – we build a comfort cocoon to block away anything unpleasant or unsavoury. We keep ourselves busy, frenetically busy (whether that involves overworking or vegging out in front of a television) – we will do almost anything to avoid thinking about life and, more importantly, death and what awaits us there. We are scared of losing our friends, our families, our pets, our homes, our standing in life. We are scared of being nothing, of being no one.

How sobering is that thought. We leave this world as we entered it. Whether a billionaire or a pauper, we go into the grave without a sausage. We are launched into infinity as a soul, nothing more or less. If we are religious, we may hope for a heaven full of pleasure and joy, or admit that we're more likely to end up being punished for our misdemeanours. I don't know the answer to that one – nobody really does. It's also asking the wrong question. The real value of pondering death is to ask how you should live your life.

I'm going to ask you to move past that delusion and fear, and to think about death. Not just any death either, I want you to think about your own death. It's not being maudlin or melo-dramatic – it's actually a sure-fire way of putting your life into perspective, of figuring out what is really important, what matters.

Death as a lesson for life

Ask almost anyone who has survived a serious illness, had a life-threatening accident or a near-death experience and they will all say the same thing: coming close to death made them truly appreciate the life they have and made them determined to live each year, each day, each *minute* as if it really mattered. I have dear friends who have cancer and say it is the best thing that has ever happened to them, as it has made them realise how incred-ible life really is and how often and how foolishly we tend to waste it. We could all learn from that. For if we choose to ignore death, there is nothing to remind us that life is precious. The spiritual teacher Denise Linn talks candidly about how she felt when she was told she had cancer:

> One day it hit me. I'd been waiting my whole life for my real life to begin. It seemed that there was always some future goal that I had to fulfil before my real life began. Consequently I never really relaxed and I always postponed my heart's desires. Confronted with the possibility of death, I suddenly realised that *this* is my life. It *has* begun. I realised there wasn't a pathway, filled with requirements you have to meet, to get to fulfilment. Happiness is how you experience each moment.

Truly none of us can tell when we will die. The first lesson of death is that we should live our lives as though every minute mattered. We should ensure that our lives have meaning; that, when we do come to die, we can look back over our lives with joy and satisfaction and peace rather than with regret and anger and sadness. If this idea catches your imagination, I'd recommend you read Stephen Levine's *A Year to Live*, a truly wonderful book about living without regret. He tried living each day as if it were his last, and found he lived life as he had never lived it before. As he says, 'Why wait for a terminal diagnosis? None of us can afford to put this work off any longer because almost no one knows the day on which the last year begins.'

One year

Think about it, if you had only one year to live, what would you do differently?

- What would you want to do with that year? What would be most important? What would not be important?
- Are there things you have always wanted to do but have put off? Review your life. Is there anything you regret not doing? Anything you always wanted to do? Why not think about doing it now?

- What job would you have really loved? Would you give up your work or change your job?
- Are there people you love but have lost touch with? Write letters to all those people you love and cherish. Tell them how important they have been to you. Tell them what you appreciate about them. Maybe you should send these letters now, before it's too late.
- With whom would you spend that year? Whom would you see more; whom would you see less? Whom could you help in this last year? Who could benefit from your time, your energy, your money? Why not try to help them now?
- Are there enemies you would like to forgive? Are there any people you hold grudges against, anyone with whom you have an ongoing feud? Do you want to take this negative energy with you when you die? If not, now's the time to put things to right.
- Is there any unfinished business to which you should attend? Have you made mistakes? Could you put them right? If not, let them go, don't waste energy on them. If there's something that could be done, why put it off?
- Spend time with this and really think about it. Why wait until you only have a year? Why not put some of your thoughts into practice right now? Do you hate your job? Change it. Do you have regrets about things you never tried? Try them. Are there people you should be in touch with? Write a letter or pick up the phone. Don't leave any possibility of regret in your life. Forgive old enemies – it's not worth the energy of holding on to hate.

If you like, you can take this exercise even further. Imagine that you had only a month, a week, a day, an hour; what would be your priorities? You may be surprised with what comes up for you. Return to this exercise frequently – at the very least once a year, to make sure you keep on track. It's also a great exercise if you tend to project your hopes into the future: 'I'll be happy when ... I have that new job/bigger house/ideal relationship/perfect body', and so on. We all do it, but focusing on the really important things that are in your life right now can put your life into perspective.

Are you spending too much time on your work and not enough with your children? Do you take your partner, your parents, your friends for granted? Are you resisting enjoying life because you're waiting to lose a few pounds? Don't wait too long – it might be too late. Use the thought of death to create life – live consciously, enjoy every moment, don't have regrets. Try not to put things off indefinitely. I'm not suggesting we all go out on a giant shopping spree, or pack up work or ditch a relationship. But I am suggesting, once again, that you think about what is really important.

Don't imagine you have limitless time. If your work doesn't work for you, look at changing it. If your relationships aren't serving you well, ask yourself why. Maybe it is time to move on, but equally it may just be time for more honesty, more communication. Do it now, don't let it fester. Before you know it you might be old and bitter, regretting a lifetime of wasted opportunities.

Annabel shifted her entire life this way. She had bought into the 'perfection culture' and insisted her life would come on-line when she finally managed to lose 9 kilos (20 pounds). Having tried the 'year to live' exercise she decided that she couldn't wait her entire life to get together the willpower or find the ideal diet. She joined a dating agency and soon met a man who loved her, curves and all. They married, had children and she retrained as a complementary therapist. Five years on, she's blissfully happy. The final irony? She's lost all the weight without even thinking about it.

What is death?

Do you remember the time before you were born? It's highly unlikely.

Death is simply another transition, like birth, from one existence to another. Tibetan Buddhism has charted the terrain of death to a degree unsurpassed by any other religion and it has a lot to teach us. According to the Tibetans there are actually six principal *bardos* or transition periods:

1. Life
2. Sleep and dreaming
3. Meditation
4. Dying
5. Instrinsic radiance
6. Becoming or rebirth

In fact, we spend our entire lives moving through transitions. There are constant small births and deaths: the start or end of a relationship; leaving an old job and starting a new one; the welcoming of a child or pet; the onset and end of illness, and so on. Nature provides us with the perfect example: the year moves through change from fresh beginnings to ripeness, to decay and finally death. Then the whole wonderful cycle begins again. If we see that life is an endless cycle of birth, maturation, death and rebirth it gives us the sense that our lives are not finite.

It pays to look on the *bardos* as moments of opportunity and potential – at every point of transition we have the wonderful opportunity of change. We can transform ourselves as often as we wish. Every night you go to sleep as one person and wake up another: take advantage of that. Every time you go into meditation, you start afresh. Yet another reason to bring meditation into your everyday life.

Facing fear

We all have pretty much the same fears. The only difference is how we face them. If we shy away from them, they grab the opportunity to grow, huge and faceless in our subconscious. If we face them bravely and squarely, they can be a stepping stone to huge growth. This lesson, although it seems wildly esoteric, is also a wonderful counterbalance to overload. It knocks out anxiety and helps you reframe your life.

Grow through facing your fears

Spend five minutes a day solidly facing your fears.

- Start with your small everyday fears. Observe your fears, watch them – realise that many of them are unnecessary or mere indulgences.
- Now move on to the big fears. What is your greatest fear? What is the worst thing that you could imagine happening to you?
- Why would it be so awful? See if you can reduce your fears down to manageable proportions. Most come down to a fear of lack of security (losing possessions, home, job); lack of love (losing dear ones, not having relationships); lack of face or status (making a fool of yourself, appearing stupid).
- The key is to remember the ebb and flow of energy. We are energetic beings living in an energetic world. When people die they do not really leave us; they are just no longer in their physical, gross, material bodies. We cannot reach out and hug them bodily but they can still touch our hearts. If you lost everything, the universe might have some new lesson for you. Many people find that, in retrospect, it can be a huge push towards growth.

Before you were born

If the idea of death still frightens you, think about this question: who were you before you were born? Where were you? Look into a small baby's eyes and there is usually something strange and knowing in them – if only they could tell us what they have seen, whence they have come. We've all been through birth: we survived. We came from somewhere into this body, this life – and we will depart from this body, this life, back to that place. The mystery is that we cannot remember.

Try this exercise – it can be quite powerful. It is also a good opportunity to review your life, seeing clearly what has worked and what hasn't. It is quite safe. Generally your subconscious will not let you access more material than you can handle comfortably. However, if at any point in this exercise you feel uncomfortable or upset, bring yourself back to full waking awareness. Stamp your feet to ground yourself and have a hot drink and something to eat. If this happens or if you know you have had a traumatic past, you may feel more comfortable doing this exercise under the guidance of a therapist.

Going back

1. Find a place where you won't be disturbed and where you can be comfortable and warm. Lie down and relax your body, checking that each part is relaxed – from the top of your head to your toes (not forgetting the shoulders, jaw, hands and all those places you know you collect tension).

2. Focus on your breath, just watching it for a few minutes. Notice how gradually it becomes slower and calmer, slower and deeper. Start breathing into your solar plexus (just above your navel) and notice how that feels. As you breathe in, know you are taking in new life and energy.

As you breathe out, allow yourself to let go of all your fear – imagine your anxieties dispersing like leaves in the wind.

3. When you feel quite relaxed and are breathing slowly and deeply, start to go back through your life. Review where you are now – what you are doing, whom you are with, how you feel. Then slowly scroll back through your adult life – don't dwell or judge, just review.

4. Take yourself back to your teenage years. Then to your childhood. What do you remember? What was important? Can you recall your first day at school? Where was your first home? How far back can you remember?

5. When you can no longer remember, start to imagine. Imagine yourself as a toddler, as a baby. If you have seen photographs, put yourself into them. Pretend you remember.

6. You are lying in your pram. Now go back further still. You are being born. You are being pushed down through the birth canal, squeezed and pressed into life. You emerge into the world and open your mouth to breathe – and out comes your first scream. Stay with this for a while – how does it feel?

7. Now go back further. You are in the womb, warm, enclosed, surrounded by the gentle waters of the amniotic fluid. You hear your mother's heartbeat above you, the gurgling of her stomach, the sway of her walk. As you float you can remember all manner of things – you can easily go back still further to a time when you were not even in physical form.

8. You are in the other place. How does it feel? How do you feel? Spend some time just being in this pure energy form. Feel the freedom.

9. Now remember why you decided to come back to earth, to a physical form. From a distance you see your parents-to-be. What made you choose them? What lessons did you all need to learn? Your parentage was no accident – it was a conscious decision. So why did you make it? Stay with this thought for some time – it may give you some very valuable insights.

10. When you feel you have learnt all you can, slowly bring your awareness back to your breath. Become aware of the room around you – your body lying on the floor. Hear the sounds around you. Gently open your eyes. Lie still for a few moments then slowly get up and stamp your feet. You may want to have a warm drink and a biscuit to ground you completely. Write down your experiences and any insights.

Realising that you *decided* to be born, that you *decided* on your parents and your situation in life, can be very liberating. Once again we have to realise that we are in control of our own lives, our own destinies. We have to take responsibility. Seemingly terrible things may have happened to us but at some level we decided to go through these experiences. We wanted to learn. What lessons are you here to learn? Will you ensure they are learnt before you die or will you miss the opportunity?

The more we face our fears and confront our own deaths, the more we will find we live. The more we make conscious decisions about how to live our lives with purpose and meaning, the less overloaded we become.

Chapter 18

The five extra secrets of a stress-free life

I want to suggest five further simple, yet unusual, ways of moving away from stress and overload. They are incredibly effective and really can reframe the way you see and react to your life. I firmly believe that if everyone made the effort to practise these (or even one or two of them) the world would not only be less stressful but also a much more pleasant place in which to live.

Secret #1: gratitude

I'm big on gratitude. It's a boon to anyone who's overloaded, particularly if your personal problem areas lie around status, perfection and the accumulation of stuff. Being grateful tells your psyche that you already have enough, that you're fine just as you are, that the world is a generous and kind and abundant place. It pulls you easily and effortlessly into the present, away from the depression of the past and the anxiety of the future. It naturally and simply focuses on the positive.

At the end of each and every day, make a list of ten things for which you are grateful. No matter how awful your day, there have to be some things that were good, that went right or, at the very least, didn't go as badly as you expected. For example, your child gave you a gorgeous hug, the bus was on time, your boss didn't bawl you out ... You get the idea?

If your life seems truly unbearable, then I'm going to suggest an idea that is as old as the world – think of someone worse off than yourself. So you could be grateful that you have health, shelter, food, and so on. Be *very* grateful that you live in an extraordinarily comfortable world. Shift your focus, stop noticing the bad and realise how much good is already in your life.

Don't leave gratitude to bedtime either. Throughout the day, be ready and willing to notice wonderful, lovely, surprising things for which you can be grateful. Sarah Ban Breathnach is the author of a fabulous book called *Simple Abundance*. In it she suggests you have 'gratitude moments' throughout the day. It could simply be the smell of freshly cooked muffins, the ray of sunlight that falls across your desk, the warm, loving email from a dear friend. Notice them, appreciate them, send out a word of thanks. Gratitude. I've done this ever since reading her book many years ago – and I still do it today, and every day.

Please don't dismiss gratitude. It is truly life-transforming.

Secret #2: service

When we're overloaded, as we've seen, we rarely have time for anyone else other than ourselves. Our families and friends suffer and so the concept of service, of helping strangers, may seem ridiculous. Yet service follows on from gratitude. As Arthur Jeon, author of *City Dharma* says, 'There are all sorts of ways to remind ourselves of how blessed we are. One of them is to volunteer, whether informally or formally.' Service – volunteering – puts your life and your overload into perspective.

Interestingly, service not only helps other people it also makes you feel good about yourself. Richard Lawrence points to a recent study by the politics department at Essex University. 'What makes people really happy is doing something for others,' he says. 'It's a finding which is 100 per cent in line with the ancient Indian philosophy of Karma.'

Helping others

There are a million-and-one ways you can help. My lawyer friends regularly do *pro bono* work, using their skills to help people who could never normally afford their services. Some people act as mentors to young people, some teach reading skills to adults who never learnt at school. Some people work in charity shops, or get their hands dirty on environmental schemes. Some befriend an old person, or raise money for charity, either by shaking a can or trekking around the world.

We are, at base, still tribal people – we did not evolve to be solitary hermits, but members of sociable, mutual helping clans, tribes, communities. When we make some kind of contribution, we naturally feel more connected, more valued. Our lives have a point. In turn, this makes us feel far less stressed and overloaded.

If you feel that, at the moment, you're too overloaded to commit your time, you can still serve in a small way, on a daily basis. Taking a hot drink or a glass of water to a stressed-out colleague is service. So is holding the bus for someone running furiously for it. Remember the huge movement regarding the idea of 'random acts of kindness'? Things you do for people who will never know you personally? There are so many opportunities to make someone else's overload that bit more bearable.

Secret #3: musing

Of course sitting and staring out the window or gazing at a fire is anathema in our time-driven world. Yet musing is one way of putting margins back into our lives. It's not as structured as meditation: you can muse any time, any place, anywhere, for however long you like. It involves doing nothing, letting your mind float free.

Jo Pickering of The Retreat Company says, 'If we could just realise that to do less is to achieve more. Inspiration comes in an instant, not from struggle or putting more hours in the office.' She's spot-on. Many of my best ideas have come when I stopped trying to find solutions but allowed my mind to float, in freeform. The key is to allow your mind to go where it will, to range far and wide, to muse.

Some of our greatest authors find their inspiration by doing nothing much at all. Novelist Rose Tremain admits to spending hours 'staring out of the window' when beginning a new book. Julie Myerson, on the other hand, stares at a blank wall, waiting for an idea to strike.

Palming

If the idea of doing absolutely nothing is simply too uncomfortable right now, have a small prop. Try palming, which is stress relieving in itself.

1. Simply lean your elbows on to your desk or table.
2. Place the palms of your hands over your eyes and allow your head to relax into your hands.
3. Muse. Stay like this for at least two minutes, longer if you can. It's a great exercise if you're stuck in front of a computer screen all day.

Silence is a great ally for musing. If you always surround yourself with noise, then musing isn't so easy. Turn off the sound. Give your ears a break. Let your brain breathe. Listen to the silence. Then notice that it's not really silent at all – use your ears, really listen. It's aural musing.

Secret #4: creativity

In my ideal world, everyone would have some form of creativity in his or her life. Psychologists now recognise that the simple unfettered enjoyment of art, dance, writing and song offers a release from tension, a way of working with your emotions and a means of challenging and processing limiting beliefs. I am a passionate advocate of the arts as therapy and feel it is a crying shame that very few GPs refer patients to the therapeutic arts – i.e. art therapy, dance therapy and music therapy. If there were more freeform expression of creativity, there would be less overload.

Let's look at a few examples:

Sound therapy

A great mood-shifter, sound therapy is an instant, easy way to release stress and tension. Simple strategies can get you started and are also quick-fire stress-relievers.

- **Humming** really helps you calm down. Simply sit quietly and hum very gently. Feel the hum resonating through your body. Where can you feel it? Notice any changes if you alter the note of the hum.
- **Sighing and groaning** If you're feeling irritable and tense, try an elongated, noisy sigh or some deep groaning. Forget about being polite – really let go.
- **Singing** Try singing the different vowel sounds – aaah, eeeeh, iiii, oooh, uuuh. Where do you feel them in your body? How do they make you feel?

- **Mantras** Play with a mantra – it needn't be *Ohm* or any-thing spiritual – simply sing positive statements. If you're feeling tense, try singing, 'I'm calm, I'm calm'; if you need to feel more assertive try, 'I can say no' or 'I have a right to be heard.'

Writing

Psychologists have long recommended we keep journals to record our daily thoughts, claiming that writing our inner-most thoughts and feelings, uncensored, can help our emotional growth and relieve stress. It doesn't matter if what you write is absolute rubbish, embarrassing, fanciful or whatever ... Nobody else ever needs to see it. Work quickly, so you don't have time to censor yourself. Try these exercises to get started:

Desert island

Imagine you are marooned on the best kind of desert island. It's beautiful and safe, with plenty of food, water and shelter. Write about the following:

1. What and whom would you miss the most? Why?
2. What and whom wouldn't you miss and why?
3. Which three things would be your desert island objects (excluding electronic gadgets such as TV, computer or phone).
4. What would be your one desert island book?
5. How would you live from day to day? Would you be able to cope with being alone? How would you do it?

Flow-writing

Start with one of these sentences and then just let your pen go where it will.

- 'For the first time in my life I …'
- 'In my heart of hearts I really wanted to …'
- 'It's been many years since …'
- 'My deepest fear is that …'
- 'Nobody ever knew that …'

After you have written each piece, underline any sentences, phrases and words that catch your attention. You might find that one of these phrases or words is the impetus for a fresh bout of flow-writing.

Dance therapy

Dancing is great exercise. It's also a wonderful form of stress relief. It really doesn't matter which kind of dance you choose – if you have always fancied floating around a ballroom, start now. If serene circle-dancing sounds suitable, join a circle (it's blissfully calming). If, on the other hand, you fancy kicking up a storm with salsa, Irish jigging or Ceroc, then go for it.

Of course it need not be any kind of organised dance – you may feel able just to go with the flow, to let the rhythm take you. However, most of us have lost the knack. That's why some dance forms have been specifically designed to produce a deep therapeutic effect on mind and body. Look out for workshops on Life Dance (Five Rhythms) and Biodanza – two wonderful forms. Try this exercise to experience a taste of Biodanza.

Biodanza

1. Walk around the room, or garden, getting in touch with your body. Feel your feet connecting firmly with the ground; let your arms swing naturally and keep your head up high. Gradually let your movements become easier, more relaxed, more exuberant.

2. Put on music with a strong but fluid melody. Dance in any way you choose, but keep aware of your chest and heart area and dance 'into' that area.

3. Change the music for something with a solid firm rhythm. Dance again, but this time letting your movements be governed by your pelvic region, the area around and below your hips.

4. Keep with rhythmic music, and play with finding your 'own' dance. Forget notions of what dancing *should* look like; don't worry about proper steps or movements. Allow the music to dance you – you might end up jumping in the air, or rolling on the floor; it doesn't matter.

Art therapy

This is my own personal favourite, my sanity-saver. Once again, it's not about being an expert. Go to an art shop and see which materials attract you. Don't censor your choice – one woman I met found she worked best painting on glass.

You don't have to make pretty or lifelike pictures but rather simply pick up your paintbrush and see what happens. Sit quietly and breathe deeply before painting. Then just see what appears on the paper. You may not even paint anything recognisable. Some people simply use colour, or shapes, or symbols. Others don't use paintbrushes – they prefer to splat paint on with their hands, or fingers, or arms. You may find it's easier to paint with your non-dominant hand (so if you're left handed, try using your right hand, and vice versa). Or shut your eyes while you paint. Or (if you have got into dance with the previous pages) dance as you paint. Afterwards try 'talking to your picture'. Write a commentary or simply scribble a letter to your painting. Ask it questions – it might answer. It sounds nuts but it does seem to work.

Secret #5: forgiveness

Just as decluttering our physical space liberates the mind, so does detoxing our interior space. Holding on to negative emotions clutters your psyche; it drags you down, clogs up your life. When you can let go and forgive you will find the world a much easier place in which to live, you will find being yourself a nicer experience. Once again, it comes down to being free to live in the present. Clinging on to negative emotions means hanging on to the past, so you can never fully enjoy the Now.

On a spiritual level forgiveness is one of the purest, most beautiful human responses. It recognises that behind every power-crazy boss is an insecure child; behind every jealous partner is someone terrified of loss, unsure of his or her attractiveness. Bullies are cowards, they fight to prevent their weakness showing through. Many people are horribly damaged in this world. If you fight negativity with negativity, everyone loses. If you counter negativity with positivity, the charge dissipates.

Take time to look deeply at your relationships and heal any that are painful or unpleasant. If you find this hard, it might be worth looking into some form of psychotherapy or practising the two-chairs technique, explained in Chapter 13: Ego, self-esteem, the Self and the soul, to understand the other person's point of view. Ask yourself how much you perhaps contributed to the situation. Let go of any old grievances. Maybe write letters to people – you don't even have to send them (you might want to have a ritual in which you burn them and release the negativity). On the other hand, it might be very healing to send them.

Tonglen

A Buddhist meditation practice, *Tonglen* is a powerful way to rid yourself of any negative and toxic emotions that may be clogging your soul – such as anger, jealousy, hate and fear. Sue Weston taught it to me, and I have found it incredibly useful – and passed it on to many people.

1. Sit comfortably either on a chair or on the floor with your back straight.
2. Allow yourself to become aware of your breathing. Just observe your breath for about five minutes or try counting 21 out-breaths.
3. Now visualise someone you love dearly in front of you. As you breathe in, breathe into yourself any pain, upset and anger they might be feeling. Allow yourself to open up to them totally and without stinting.
4. As you breathe out, breathe all that is good in you into them. Imagine their pain and suffering transforming inside you into healing light – you are not holding their suffering, merely transforming it.
5. Repeat this for about five minutes.
6. You can repeat this with as many people as you like. Keep practising until you are proficient and can feel the healing energy inside you at will.
7. When you have perfected this you are ready for the next step. Now, instead of someone you love, imagine someone you dislike or even hate in front of you. Now transform their pain and anger and give them back the pure healing light of love.

Following on from this, I'd suggest you read a lovely book

called *The Gentle Art of Blessing* by Pierre Pradervand. In it the author shows how sending out blessings to people you know, people you don't know, people you like, people you hate, and especially to yourself, can be a powerful force in healing overload and stress.

Keep an open mind and do try the five secrets. I think you may well be surprised at what happens.

Chapter 19

Set yourself free

Come on, wake up, it's a beautiful world out there! If you weren't overloaded, what would you be doing? Stop, right now, and jot down your ideal 'to do' list. How would it run? What delicious tasks and activities would you include on that list? Starting work on your own business? Hugging your child? Making love with your partner? Having lunch with friends and laughing your heads off? An hour at the gym? An afternoon in the garden? Now stop believing it can only be wishful thinking – and make some changes.

Our society loves and promotes overload – there is no doubt about that. But what's to say you have to buy into that madness? If your friends and colleagues want to continue killing themselves and wrecking their relationships in search of a poisoned chalice of debt, stress and status, let them. But who says you have to plunge, lemming-like, after them? Who says you have to sacrifice your health, your happiness, to fit in with the crowd? Who says you have to live in the right kind of house, wear the right kind of clothes, do the right kind of work, send your children to the right kinds of school? Who says you need ten credit cards, flash holidays and the latest fashions and gizmos? Why should other people demand what *you* do with *your* life? It is your life – remember – and you can choose how you live it.

This book has given you a whole clutch of tools to free you from overload. Whether or not you use them is entirely up to you. Whether or not you buy into overload is up to you.

....

Leave overload behind

If you strengthen your ego and self-esteem enough you will be able to set clear boundaries and make wise choices. If you learn to live more in the present, letting go of grudges, resentment and anxiety, stress is far less likely to hold sway in your world. If you make space in your life for love, friendship, community and creativity, you won't be lured into the status, perfection and overwork traps. Above all, if you can find your authentic Self, you simply won't allow overload to bother you.

....

Behind all the glitter and gloss of modern life hides a small, unpretentious yet vital task. Your ultimate purpose as a human being is to discover your true Self, to find the meaning for your individual life. You need to get in touch with the Self that lies beyond the ego, your true inner Self that is wise, and loving, and balanced, and unique. Finding your true Self is tough hard soul work. You're unlikely to discover it at some weekend workshop; it won't jump out at you when you're lying on your Gucci yoga mat; it won't magically appear if you tie a piece of red string around your wrist. There is no quick-fix method to discover your soul. It's tough work, every-day work. You have to keep questioning yourself, asking 'what is the actual meaning of my life?'

The meaning of life can come in the smallest, simplest things. A dear friend, the writer Joanne Leonard, tells me that there is a Navajo word *hozh'q* (pronounced hoe-shk), which means the beauty of life, as seen or created by a person. Jo says:

If you ask us to think about our wealth, we might think about our bank balance or our house. But if you ask a Navajo, the answer might possibly be the number of songs they know, especially the ones they made up themselves. Beauty is a way to live, not something that exists on the surface of things, and you can find it anywhere – *hozh'q* grows inside humans who perceive the universe as it should be, in all its glory, and then spreads outwards. So every time we make a nice sentence or arrange flowers in a nice way, or hum a little tune we are practising *hozh'q* and making the universe richer.

Our celebrity worship

The true reason why so many of us are fixated on celebrity is due to a lack of meaning in our lives, a lack of sense of our own unique wonderful Self. As humans we are hard-wired to seek a part of ourselves that is beyond the ego, greater than the ego, our own individual 'star' essence. If you can't or won't find that within yourself, you will end up projecting it outwards on to somebody else. In the past we worshipped gods and goddesses, projecting various parts of our psyches on to them. Kings and queens provided a similar function, representing an external version of our own inner ruler and authority (the reason why Princess Diana was such a potent archetype for so many people was that she represented our own inner princess, our unique specialness). But now, with the power of royalty and religion breaking down for so many people, all we are left with is celebrity.

If we do not have a strong sense of our own Self, we need something or someone outside ourselves to admire and revere and believe in. 'What people are doing in making celebrities is trying to create gods and goddesses,' says Sarah Dening. 'Celebrities don't threaten and they don't challenge; they merely provide glamour and image.'

Next time you feel compelled to read a celebrity magazine or watch another 'celebrity special' on television, ask yourself what you are missing in your own life. How could you celebrate your own inner 'star'? What makes you such a unique individual? What is the meaning of your life? What is your purpose? How can you make a difference? Hunt for your true Self and your craving for living a second-hand life through celebrity will fade as fast as fake tan.

Society and the Self

Seeking the Self in our modern society is not easy. We may crave authenticity but it's not taught in schools. It's ignored by the media and even the self-help movement is often more concerned with having it all than true soul work. In our society, as we've seen, we are constantly being goaded to be better, to look better, to have more. We are brainwashed into following the herd, bowing to fashion, and so we move further and further away from our authentic selves, never finding inner peace. If you are not in touch with the centre of your being, nothing can ever be right. If you are off-centre, always chasing rainbows, you will never be fulfilled, contented, at peace.

But if society promotes overload so much, what can we as individuals do about it? The answer is simple: change society one person at a time. In other words, we start by changing ourselves. Remember: you can never change someone else but, by changing your own reactions and behaviour, other people around you will often change all by themselves. You are not helpless. You can make shifts. You do have a voice. Empower yourself in small ways – campaign at local levels on matters that affect your life. For example, consumer demand has brought organic food into our supermarkets. When I badgered enough people in my local area to write to our MP about the state of a dangerous road, it was widened and made safe. People working in a crowded unpleasant office took a proposal for flexi-time home-working to their bosses and now half the workforce work from their homes, fitting work in with family.

Change isn't easy. It's far easier to continue blaming our problems on society, on the 'system'. It's simpler to abnegate responsibility. Moaning, whining and complaining are far less effort than taking possibly scary or challenging steps to change your life. Yes, society is geared towards overload; it promotes it and advocates it. Yet that doesn't mean you have to cave in and accept it as given. You do have responsibility for your own life.

You can always choose your own responses. You can decide not to buy into celebrity culture, into overwork, into affluenza and presenteeism. You can choose not to keep up with the Joneses but to be your own person, secure in your own values and beliefs. You can make clear boundaries and give time to the important roles in your life, because you know what is important and what is unnecessary. You can switch off the mobile, you can turn off the TV. Choose wisely. It's up to you.

Richard Jacobs, author of *What's Your Purpose?* puts it well:

Anyone reading this is living in greater luxury than any royal person of all time. We are all kings and queens, and yet with the pressures we create in modern society we treat ourselves as slaves. Life becomes a stress to be faced or managed rather than a thrilling adventure of expansion, evolution, meaning and the discovery of the greater possibility of life. We are all born with the supreme gifts of imagination and free choice. Those two simple abilities can bring us any future we desire. All we have to do is choose our highest choice.

Follow your treasure map

As I write this last chapter of *The Overload Solution* I have come to my own, tough choice. I have decided that it's time to downshift, to allow myself more time to spend with my husband, my child and my other creative interests. We're planning to sell our big country house and buy somewhere smaller and cheaper in a nearby small town. I'm all too aware of the swift passing of time and I don't want to look back and regret lost opportunities. My treasure map shows families walking on the beach, friends laughing over lunch, an art studio, women doing yoga and aerobics, having massages and dancing – oh, and well-behaved dogs (well, one can dream!).

Make the conscious choice to climb off couch-potato Britain, USA, or wherever you may be. Recognise that if you are not being creative in your own life, you are a sitting target to be manipulated by our expectation society. Sitting passively, doing what you're told, will bring you overload, lack of meaning and a deep, *soul*-deep sense of dissatisfaction. Don't wait until you have a year to live to learn how to live. Get off the treadmill, kiss goodbye to overload. Start living your real life right now.

Bibliography

Alexander, Jane, *Spirit of the Home*, HarperCollins, 1998

Alexander, Jane, *The Five-Minute Healer*, Gaia, 2000

Aron, Elaine N., *The Highly Sensitive Person*, Broadway Books, 1996

Ball, Stefan, *The Bach Remedies Workbook*, C.W. Daniel, 1998

Breathnach, Sarah Ban, *Simple Abundance*, Bantam 1997

Bunting, Madeleine, *Willing Slaves*, HarperCollins, 2004

Chandler, Robin and Grzyb, Jo Ellen, *The Nice Factor Book*, Simon & Schuster, 1997

Crofts, Neil, *Authentic – How to Make a Living by Being Yourself*, Capstone, 2003

Crofts, Neil, *Authentic Business*, Capstone, 2005

Curtis, Mark, *Distraction*, Futuretext, 2005

De Botton, Alain, *Status Anxiety*, Hamish Hamilton, 2004

De Graaf, John, *Affluenza: The All-Consuming Epidemic*, Berrett-Koehler, 2001

Dening, Sarah, *Healing Dreams*, Hamlyn, 2004

Easterbrook, Gregg, *The Progress Paradox*, Random House, 2003

Franks, Lynn, *The Seed Handbook*, Piatkus Books, 2005

Geary, Michael, *Panchang Moon Astrology*, Thorsons, 2001

Harp, David, *The 3-Minute Meditator*, Piatkus Books, 1990

Holden, Robert, *Happiness Now!*, Hodder & Stoughton, 1998

Honoré, Carl, *In Praise of Slow*, Orion, 2004

Hoschschild, Arlie Russell, *The Time Bind: When Work Becomes*

   Home and Home Becomes Work, Owl Books, 2001

Jacobs, Richard, *What's Your Purpose?* Hodder and Stoughton, 2004

Jarow, Rick, *Creating the Work You Love*, Destiny, 1995

Jeon, Arthur, *City Dharma*, Piatkus Books, 2004

Kabat-Zinn, Jon, *Mindfulness Meditation for Everyday Life*, Piatkus Books, 1994

Kabat-Zinn, Jon, *Full Catastrophe Living*, Piatkus Books, 1990

Kabat-Zinn, Jon, *Coming To Our Senses*, Piatkus Books, 2005

Kübler-Ross, Elisabeth, *On Death and Dying*, Prentice Hall, 1997

Kübler-Ross, Elisabeth, *Life Lessons*, Simon & Schuster, 2001

Kundtz, David, *Stopping*, Conari Press, 1998

Lawrence, Richard, *Meditation: A Complete Workout for the Mind*, Mind Body Spirit Direct, 2004

Lazarides, Linda, *The Nutritional Health Bible*, Thorsons, 1997

Lazarides, Linda, *Treat Yourself with Nutritional Therapy*, Waterfall, 2000

Levine, Stephen, *A Year to Live*, Bell Tower, 1997

Lewis, Martin, *The Money Diet*, Vermilion, 2004

Linn, Denise, *Secrets & Mysteries*, Rider, 2002

Longaker, Christine, *Facing Death & Finding Hope*, Arrow, 1998

Mayne, Brian and Sangeeta, *Life Mapping*, Vermilion, 2003

McEwen, Dr Bruce, *The End of Stress as We Know it*, National Academies Press, 2002

Miller, Kevin A., *Surviving Information Overload*, Zondervan, 2004

Moore, Thomas, *Dark Nights of the Soul*, Piatkus Books, 2004

Mumford, Dr Jonn, *Death: Beginning or End?* Llewellyn, 1999

Pearsall, Paul, *Toxic Success*, Inner Ocean, 2002

Peiffer, Vera, *Total Stress Relief*, Piatkus Books, 2003

Pradervand, Pierre, *The Gentle Art of Blessing*, Cygnus, 2005

Renshaw, Ben, *Successful but Something Missing*, Rider, 2000

Reynolds, Caroline, *Spiritual Fitness*, Thorsons, 2001

St James, Elaine, *Simplify Your Life*, Hyperion, 1994

St James, Elaine, *Living the Simple Life*, Hyperion, 1996

Schwartz, Barry, *The Paradox of Choice*, HarperCollins, 2004

Shenk, David, *Data Smog*, HarperSanFrancisco, 1997

Swenson, Dr Richard A., *Margin*, Navpress, 1992

Swenson, Dr Richard A., *The Overload Syndrome*, Navpress, 1998

Toffler, Alvin, *Future Shock*, Pan, 1973

Tolle, Eckhart, *The Power of Now*, New World Library, 1999

Tysoe, Dr Maryon, *The Good Relationship Guide*, Piatkus, 1995

Vaughan, Sue, *Finding the Stillness Within in a Busy World*, C. W. Daniel, 1995

Warren, Elizabeth and Tyagi, Amelia Warren, *The Two-Income Trap*, Basic Books, 2003

Weller, Stella, *The Breath Book*, Thorsons, 1999

Williams, Nick, *The Work We Were Born to Do*, Element, 1999

Wright, Robert, *The Moral Animal*, Vintage, 1994

Wurman, Richard Saul, *Information Anxiety*, Bantam, 1990

Resources

General contact details

General sites on overload, stress, depression and anxiety, providing information and support:

American Association for Marriage and Family Therapy
www.aamft.org – advice, help and counselling for relationships.

Anxiety Information Network
www.anxietynetwork.com – informative information on anxiety disorders.

CCCS
www.cccs.co.uk – charity that gives advice and support on debt, credit cards etc.

Depression Alliance
www.depressionalliance.org

Institute of Stress Management
www.isma.org.uk or *www.isma-usa.org* – huge array of features on all aspects of stress and how to cope with it.

Job Stress Network
www.workhealth.org

Mental Health Foundation (UK)
www.mentalhealth.org.uk

Mental Health Information Center (US)
www.mentalhealth.org

Relate
www.relate.org.uk

Touching Minds
www.touchingminds.org – offers advice and information on mood disorders plus how to get help both in the UK and the USA. Excellent links to other sites.

Contributors to The Overload Solution

These contributors have excellent websites offering practical advice and/or thought-provoking features alongside their professional services:

Jonathan Chuter
A kinesiologist, healer, corporate consultant and guide.
Tel: 01225 329140

Neil Crofts and Authentic Business
www.authenticbusiness.co.uk – huge network of authentic businesses, courses, and related links.

Mark Curtis
www.distractionculture.com – thought provoking and alarming on the possibilities and dangers of digital technology.

Sarah Dening
www.sarahdening.net – offers insights into dreams and Jungian psychotherapy. Sarah also runs workshops on using your dreams to discover your true Self.

Stephanie Driver
Stephanie practises at naturopathic clinic Apotheke 20-20 in London, UK.
www.apotheke20-20.co.uk

Michael Geary
www.panchang.com – helps people make the most of their time. 'Life-change' workshops and individual consultations.

Richard Jacobs
www.one-purpose.com – looks at how people can live their greatest and most meaningful lives.

Linda Lazarides
www.health-diets.net – superb nutritional health website, packed with information.

Richard Lawrence
www.richardlawrence.co.uk – lectures and workshops on a wide variety of New Age and alternative subjects.

Brian Mayne and Sangeeta Mayne
www.liftinternational.com – coping with change; goal mapping and life mapping.

Will Parfitt
www.willparfitt.com – mind-shifting workshops, seminars and courses on psychosynthesis and Kabbalah.

Barry Schwartz, Professor of Social Theory and Social Action
www.swarthmore.edu/SocSci/bschwar1/

Jane Thurnell-Read
www.healthandgoodness.com – interesting natural health resource.

Joy Toop
Joy sells a huge range of crystals and also works as a healer.
Tel: 01643 831268

Sue Weston
www.relaxingthemind.com – workshops and retreats on qi gong, t'ai chi, anger management, meditation and general relaxation.

Lisa Wynn
Prosperity coaching.
www.prosperitycoaching.com and *www.lisawynn.com*

Retreats

Fiona Arrigo
www.fiona-arrigo.com – luxury retreats in the UK.

The Retreat Company
www.theretreatcompany.com – offering a great range of 'time out' breaks around the world.

Caroline Reynolds
www.spiritual-fitness.com – spiritual retreats in the US.

The Spirit of Life Centre
www.thespiritoflife.co.uk – wonderful retreats and healing pilgrimages in Greece.

Further contact details

Other interesting and useful organisations and people, mentioned in *The Overload Solution*:

Acts of Kindness
www.actsofkindness.org

Art therapy
www.baat.org

Biodanza
www.biodanza.co.uk

Christopher Connolly (sports psychologist)
www.sbm.co.uk

Robert Holden (psychologist)
www.happiness.co.uk

The Impact Factory
Courses in assertiveness and communication skills.
www.impactfactory.com

Arthur Jeon (author of *City Dharma*)
www.citydharma.typepad.com

Jon Kabat-Zinn
Center for Mindfulness, University of Massachusetts Medical School.
www.umassmed.edu/cfm

Life Dance
www.gabrielleroth.com

Music therapy
www.bsmt.org

National Institutes of Health Center for the Neuroscience of Fear and Anxiety at New York University
www.cns.nyu.edu/CNFA

Rockefeller University (Professor Bruce McEwen)
www.rockefeller.edu

Slow Food
www.slowfood.com

Sound therapy
www.susanlever.co.uk

World Values Survey
www.worldvaluessurvey.org

Robert Wright
www.nonzero.org – this site is fascinating. It also links to his earlier work on *The Moral Animal.*

Psychotherapists

To find a qualified psychotherapist contact:

American Counseling Association
www.counseling.org

Australian Counselling Association
www.theaca.net.au

British Association for Counselling and Psychotherapy
www.bacp.co.uk – on-line register of private therapists covering a broad spectrum of disciplines.

European Association for Counselling
www.eacnet.org

European Association for Psychotherapy
www.europsyche.org

Gestalt Therapy
www.gestaltcentre.co.uk and *www.aagt.org*

Process work
www.aamindell.net

Psychosynthesis
www.psychosynthesis.org

Transpersonal Psychology
www.transpersonalcentre.co.uk and *www.atpweb.org*

UK Council for Psychotherapy
www.psychotherapy.org.uk

Supplements

Blackmores
www.blackmores.com.au

Good source of herbals from various companies
www.iherb.com

New Chapter
www.new-chapter.com

Revital – an excellent mail order company with a huge range of supplements.
www.revital.com

Visit *www.janealexander.org* – packed with information on natural health, holistic living, detoxing, complementary therapies, and much more. You can also contact Jane through the website.

Index

achievement 153–4
adaptation 82
adaptogens 128
addictions
   to labels 120
   to spending 121
   to work 45
adrenal glands 5
adrenal overload 123
adrenalin, effects on the body 5, 6
aerobic exercise 129
affairs, online 19–20
affirmations 118
'affluenza' 37
ageing
   of the population 22–3
   premature 17
air quality 89
alcohol intake 46, 81, 125
Alexander Technique 89
allostatic overload 8
alternative practitioners 190
American Psychological Association (APA) xiv
amygdala 17
anti-depressants 46
   herbal 160
anti-stress emergency kits 96
antioxidants 124
anxiety 10, 158–60

about the future/change 34–5
   epidemic of 17–19
   as learned response 18–19
appearance, low-maintenance 72–3
arguments 93, 103–4, 107
aromatherapy 90–1, 96
Aron, Elaine N 11–12
arrogance 147
art therapy 209–10
attitudes 164–5
Authentic Movement 169–71
authenticity 168–78, 214, 216
   being authentic 171–6
   Core Statement 176–8
autoimmune disorders 11
availability 29–30

Bach flower remedies 139–41
bags 73
Baker, Sam 12
beans 125
beauty tips, no-nonsense 72–3
being alone, fear of 142
beliefs 147–9, 163
   self-limiting 154–6
Biodanza 208–9
birthdays 182–3
blood sugar levels 123
body, effect of stress on 4–7
Botton, Alain de 30

boundaries 83–4, 92, 147, 149, 151

brain 4
  chemistry 123, 159
  'fogging' 79–80
  stress and the 16–17

breathing techniques 130–1, 133

Breathnach, Sarah Ban 203

British Heart Foundation 38

'brownout' xi

Buddhism 197, 211

budgets 119

bullies 191–2

Bunting, Madeleine 45

burnout xi

caffeine 80–1, 125

calendars 66

cancer 193–4

candles 89

carbohydrates, refined 125

cars 182, 184, 185

celebrities 31, 148–9, 215–16

centaury 139

chamomile 127–8

change 34–5
  bringing about 170–1, 216–17
  preparing for 137–45

childcare, sharing 58–9

children
  overweight 38
  texting and 29–30
  as the victims of parental overload 20–1

choices 31–2, 213, 217–18
  about overload 51–2, 142
  about your pace of life 183
  limiting your 82
  'over-choice' 32
  simplifying your 183–4

cholesterol 5, 132

Chore-based Breath Count exercise 133

Christmas 182–3

Chuter, Jonathan 36–7, 170

clary sage 90

clothing, work 72

clutter, clearing out 63–5, 71, 89, 95, 184–5

coffee 80–1

collections 184, 185

comfort eating 123

communication 103–6

communities, as the victims of overload 22

commuting 95–9

Complete Breath exercise 131

Connolly, Christopher 128–9

control 30

cooking 185

cooking methods 126

coping strategies, negative xiv

Core Statement 176–8

cortisol 7
  and caffeine 80
  effects on the body 5, 6, 17
  herbal reduction of 127
  and over-weight status 37
  production cessation during sleep 38
  reducing levels through meditation 132

cosmetic surgery 33

Cosmopolitan magazine 12

counselling 159

countryside, living in the 180–1

creativity 141, 206–10
  as the victim of overload 23–4

credit cards 36, 119, 121

Crofts, Neil 169–70

Crowd Dancing exercise 98

Curtis, Mark 28

cybersex 19–20

dance therapy 208–9
'data smog' xii, 28
death 192–201
debt 36, 119, 121
defining overload 8–15, 55
delegation 56–8
demons of overload 26–38
Dening, Sarah 41, 147, 148, 149, 164, 171, 215
depression 12, 159–60
    epidemic of 17–18
Desert Island exercise 207
'desk rage' xi–xii
desks 71
diaries 66, 164, 207
    spending 118–19
    thought 152–3
diet 122–8
    comfort eating 123
    food intolerances/sensitivities 124
    organic food 124, 189
    overload 123, 125–6
    and the Slow Movement 187–8
    supplements 126–8
diet foods 126
digestive system 5
disagreements 103–4
disorganisation 70
doing nothing 191
domestic chores 57–8, 59, 190
'doormats' 139
dopamine 123
downshifting 217–18
Driver, Stephanie 17, 80, 123, 127
driving 95–6, 190

early birds 71
Easterbrook, Gregg 52
'eating elephants' 67
ego-gratification 147

egos 145–54, 160, 186–7, 191–2, 214–15
Einstein, Albert 87
elderly people 22–3
electromagnetic fields (EMFs) 89
emails 70, 79–80, 88
emotions 159
    negative 138–41, 211
    symptoms of overload 14
empathy 35, 92, 105–6, 110, 210
employees, 'addicted' 45
endorphins 4
enemies 195
energy 123
essential fatty acids (EFAs) 125
essential oils 90–1, 96
expectations 82
eye movement desensitisation reprogramming (EMDR) 160

faith 43–4
families
    assessing your 55
    assessing your relationships with 141
    goals 105
    mealtimes 189
    planning time with 68
    as the victims of overload 22
family scripts 172–3
fast food 189
fats, dietary 125–6
fear 17–18
    of being alone 142
    choosing overload instead 142
    of death 192–3, 198
    facing 198
    of the future/change 34–5, 158
feedback 14
'fight or flight' response 4–7

finances 35–6, 37, 141
  budgets 119
  debt 36, 119, 121
  detoxing your 111–21
  money and happiness 42,
    111–15, 117–18
flow-writing 208
flower remedies 139–41
food intolerances/sensitivities
  124
forgiveness 210–12
Fortune magazine 145
Franks, Lynn 169
fried food 126
friends 23, 55, 70, 83, 195
fruit 124
future, fear of the 34–5, 158
Future Foundation, The 32
'future shock syndrome' xii,
  34

gardens 185–7, 189
Geary, Michael 77, 170
geranium 91
Gestalt therapy 150
gift-giving 186
gluten 124
goal-setting 66–7
Going Back exercise 199–201
Good Housekeeping magazine 22
gratitude 202–3
greed 113
groaning 206
gurus 41–2, 44

hairstyles 72
happiness
  avoiding 162–4
  key to 158–67
  and money 42, 111–15,
    117–18
  and relationships 183

Harp, David 133
health 141
heart 5
heart disease 30
herbs
  anti-depressant 160
  culinary 126
  for stress 127–8
'highly sensitive people' 11–12
hippocampus 17
hoarders 186
hobbies 23–4, 55, 190
Holden, Robert 165
Holford, Patrick 123
holidays 46–7, 84, 182, 189
holy basil 127
Honore, Carl 187
hornbeam 139
houses 55
  decorating 33
  'house bloat' 37
  living abroad 181
  prices 35
housework 57–8, 59, 190
housing
  downshifting 179–81, 217–18
  low-maintenance 185–7
humming 206
hunter-gatherers 7
hypertension 132
hypnotherapy 160
hypothalamus 4

identity 148
illnesses 10–11, 193–4
immortalists 192
immune system 6, 10
immune-boosters, herbal 127–8
impatiens 139
Improvement and Development
  Agency for Local
  Government 23

inauthenticity 171
'infomania' 79–80
information 26–8
Information Fatigue Syndrome
(IFS) xii, 27
information overload 86–8
inner critics 152–3
insomnia
herbal remedies for 128
and stress 38
inspiration 205
International Journal of
Neuroscience 130
Internet 27
adultery on the 19–20
reducing the time you spend
on 79–80, 185
as time stealer 70

Jacobs, Richard 170, 217
Jarow, Rick 169
Jeon, Arthur 44, 203
job security 28
Journal of Sleep Research 29–30
Jung, C. G. 24
junk food 126

Kabbalah 44
Kinsey 190

label addiction 120
Lancet (journal) 129
lavender 91
Lawrence, Richard 113, 203–4
LeDoux, Joseph 35
lemon balm 128
Leonard, Joanne 214
letting go 85
Levine, Stephen 194
Lewis, David 27
libraries 186
life maps 151–2
life transitions 197

lifestyle 37–8
Linn, Denise 194
liquorice 128
listening skills 105–6
liver 5
living abroad 181
loans, home-equity 36
Looking at Your Life exercise
54–5
Lottery winners 111
lungs 6

McCreddie, Laura 43
McEwen, Bruce 8, 18–19
MacLeod, Sheila 176, 178
magazines 78–9, 185
magnesium 127
make-up 72
mandarin 91
mantras 132, 207
marijuana 46
Marmot, Michael 30
Marriott hotels 94
materialism 36–7, 184, 185,
186–7
maximisers 33
Mayne, Brian 32, 183
'me time' 24–5, 71
meaning 24, 214–15
personal 44–5
media embargoes 78–9
meditation 132–3, 197
exercises 163–4
meetings, inefficient 70
Mental Health Foundation 23
mental symptoms of overload
13–14
Microsoft 45
Miller, Kevin A. 86
mind, effects of stress on 6
Mindful Walking exercise 98–9
mindfulness 133
Mindfulness Meditation 163–4

Miracle Question exercise
    113–15, 143–4, 182
mitochondria 123
mobile phones, turning off 75–6
moment, living in the 158–9,
    160–7
money 35–6, 37
    and happiness 42, 111–15,
        117–18
'money partners' 120
'more', pursuit of 112–13, 115
muscles 6
music 96
musing 205–6
Myerson, Julie 205

nails 72
nannies 58–9
National Institutes of Health 18
naturopaths 126–7
Navajo Indians 214–15
near-death experiences 193–4
Neuro-Linguistic Programming
    (NLP) 153–4, 160
New York Times (newspaper) 27
'Newness of Life' game 165
newspapers, embargoes 78
niceness 92–3
night owls 71
no
    ability to say 146
    inability to say 70–1, 139
    learning to say 61, 93
noradrenalin 5
norepinephrine 123
nurseries 21
nutritional supplements 126–8
nutritional therapists 126–7
nuts 124

oak 139
oats 127

oils
    dietary 125
    essential 90–1, 96
olive 140
onset of overload 9–12
Orange 45
organic food 124, 189
organisation 65–6
'over-choice' 32
overload solution 135–218
    authenticity 168–78
    beliefs 147–9, 154–6
    creativity 206–10
    and death 192–201
    doing nothing 190–1
    downshifting 179–83
    and the ego 146–54
    forgiveness 210–12
    gratitude 202–3
    the key to happiness 158–67
    musing 205–6
    and the persona 149–50
    preparing for change 137–45
    simplification 183–7
    slow down 187–90
    volunteering/service 203–4
overload-busting strategies
    49–133
    alcohol intake reduction 81
    boundary setting 83–4
    clearing out clutter 63–5
    cutting caffeine 80–1
    cutting commitments 55–61
    delegation 56–8
    financial detox 111–21
    friendships 83
    goal-setting 66–7
    Internet diets 79–80
    letting go 85
    limiting choices 82
    Looking at Your Life exercise
        54–5

media embargoes 78–9
organisation 65–6
planning 67–70
questions to ask yourself 52–3
reframing stress 61–3
relationship MOT 100–10
sharing tasks 56, 58–60
shedding tasks 56, 60–1
stress-reduction 122–33
turning off mobiles 75–6
unplugging the television 76–7
for work 86–99
Your Life as a Circle exercise 53–4
overweight people 37–8
overworking 28–9

palming 205
parents, cold/unloving 116
Parfitt, Will 73–4
passionflower 128
past, living in the 160–1
Peiffer, Vera 61
perfectionism 32–4, 85, 109, 140
persona 149–50
personal growth, work as 44–6
Pert, Candace 159, 161
petitgrain 91
pets 185
physical exercise 128–30
physical symptoms of overload 13
Pickering, Jo 160, 205
planning 67–70
plants, anti-toxin 89
Playing Oprah exercise 155–6
positivity 41–2, 62, 166–7
possessions 36–7, 184, 185, 186–7
posture, seated 89
Pradervand, Pierre 212
pranyama (breathing technique) 130
presenteeism 30, 94–5
proactive behaviour 71
processed foods 126
productivity, and work hours 94
Provigil 29
psyche 146, 157
psychotherapy 143, 159, 160, 210
public transport 96–9
pulses 125

qi gong 97, 130

reflection 164
reframing 61–3
regret 82
anticipated 32
relationships
communication and 103–6
family 100–6
knowing what you want from 103
MOT 100–10
partners 106–10
and perfectionism 109
questions about 141
relationship circle 101
as the victims of overload 19–20, 100
religion 43–4
Renshaw, Ben 169
retreats 138, 191
Reynolds, Caroline 155
Rhodiola rosea 160
Riccio, Massimo 46
Right Now Mindfulness Meditation 163–4
road rage 95–9
Robbins, Anthony 41
rock water 140
Roman chamomile 91
Roy, Sondra 41

Sabbath 188
St James, Elaine 138, 144
St John's wort 160
salt 125, 126
sandalwood 91
Schumacher, E F 183
Schwartz, Barry 31
scleranthus 140
scripts, family 172–3
seeds 124
selective serotonin reuptake
    inhibitors (SSRIs) 46
Self 146, 150, 156–7, 169, 187,
    214–17
self-discipline, lack of 71
self-esteem 42, 146, 148, 151–4,
    156, 214
self-help books 40
senses 6
Sentence for Life exercise 73–4
serotonin 123
sex 107, 190
    txtsex/cybersex 19–20
sharing tasks 56, 58–60
Shenk, David 28
shopping 185
Siberian ginseng 128
sighing 206
silence 191, 206
singing 206
skin
    caring for your 72–3
    effects of stress on the 6
sleep
    herbal remedies for 128
    lack of and overload 38
    reducing the amount people
        need 29
Slow Movement 187–90
Solution Therapy 113
soul 146
sound therapy 206–7

soya 125
space, sacred/relaxing 137–8
spam 28, 88
spas 39–40
'spaving' 36
spending
    as addiction 121
    diaries 118–19
    patterns of 116–18
spirituality 157, 183
    assessing your 55
    bogus 43–4
    as victim of overload 24–5
sprouts 125
status 30–1
stress 3–8, 15
    anti-stress emergency kit 96
    chronic xiv
    definition of xiv, 3–7
    effect on the body 4–7
    and insomnia 38
    reframing 61–3
    as safety response 3–7
    and success 7–8
    and unhappiness 7–8
stress hormones 5
stress response
    inability to shut down 7–8
    malfunctioning 16–17
stress-management industry
    39–42
stress-reduction 122–33
    breathing 130–1
    diet 122–8
    meditation 132–3
    physical exercise 128–30
    what does not work 39–47
stretching 71
subconscious mind 199
    accessing 143–4
    power of 166
success, focusing on 153–4

sugar 125
sweet chestnut 140
symptoms of overload 12–15
   emotional 14
   feedback from others 14
   mental 13–14
   physical 13

Tantra 190
telephone calls 70, 186
   see also mobile phones
television 76–7
texts 29–30
This Moment exercise 165
thought diaries 152–3
thyroid gland 5
Tibetan Buddhism 197
time 28–9
   management of 64, 67, 69–70
   savers 71
   Sentence for Life exercise
      73–4
   stealers 70–1
   winning back 64–74
'to do' lists 69, 213
Toffler, Alvin 32, 34
Tonglen (meditation practice)
   211
Tongue-block Breath Mediation
   133
trampolines 129
treasure maps 143–4, 217–18
Tremain, Rose 205
'two chairs' technique 150, 210
txtsex 19–20

UK Sleep Alliance 38
underload syndrome 180–1
utility bills 119

values 148, 149, 163
vegetables 124
vervain 140

victims of overload 19–25
   children 20–1
   communities 22
   creativity 23–4
   families 22
   relationships 19–20, 100
   spirituality 24–5
visualisation 97–8, 211
vitamin B complex 127
volunteering/service 23, 203–4

walking, mindful 98–9
Wall Street Journal 29, 37
weekends 84
weight loss 196
Weston, Sue 132, 211
'what you want', understanding
   144–5
wheat 124
white chestnut 140
whole grains 124
Williams, Nick 169
withania 127
work
   assessing your beliefs about
      172–3
   assessing your job 54
   authentic 169–76
   clothing 72
   commuting 95–9
   discovering what suits you
      173–4
   handling difficult people at
      91–2
   hating your job 168–9, 172
   ideal 174, 175–6
   inefficient meetings 70
   information overload at 86–8
   language of 174–5
   learning to be less nice at
      92–3
   making your workplace a
      sanctuary 89–91

overload-busting strategies
86–99
overworking 28–9
as personal growth 44–6
presenteeism 30, 94–5
relaxing after 81
setting boundaries at 83–4, 92
stretch breaks 71
telephone calls at 70
work hours, and productivity 94

'worst-case scenario' game 63
Wright, Robert 7
writing 207–8
Wu Qi exercise 97
Wynn, Lisa 112, 116, 154–5, 171

ylang-ylang 91
yoga 43, 129, 130, 133
Your Life as a Circle exercise
53–4